HOW TO LAND AN A330 AIRBUS

Also by James May
James May's Magnificent Machines
James May's 20th Century
Car Fever

HOW TO LAND AN A330 AIRBUS

AND OTHER VITAL SKILLS FOR THE MODERN MAN

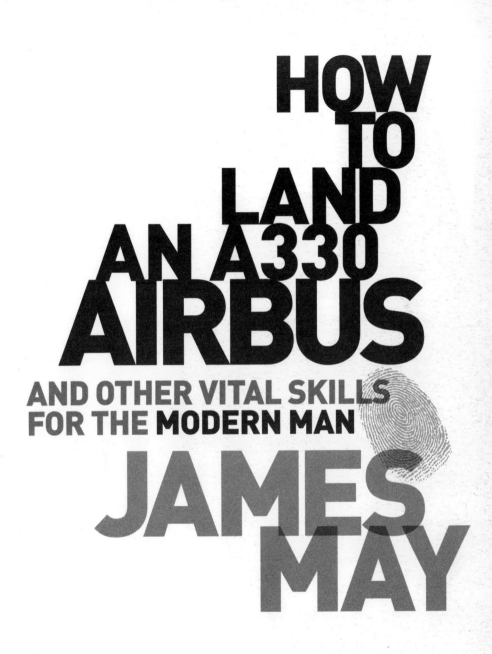

JAMES MAY

HODDER &
STOUGHTON

Neither the author nor the publisher can accept any legal responsibility or liability for any harm arising from the techniques, advice or situations described in this book.

First published in Great Britain in 2010 by Hodder & Stoughton
An Hachette UK company

A CIP catalogue record for this title is available from the British Library.

Hardback ISBN 978 0 340 99456 6
Trade Paperback ISBN 978 0 340 99457 3

Designed by Bobby Birchall, Bobby&Co.
Illustrations by Mike Garland
Printed and bound by Clays Ltd, St Ives plc

Hodder & Stoughton policy is to use papers that are natural, renewable and recyclable products and made from wood grown in sustainable forests. The logging and manufacturing processes are expected to conform to the environmental regulations of the country of origin.

Hodder & Stoughton Ltd
338 Euston Road
London NW1 3BH

www.hodder.co.uk

To Dad, for forcing me to build my own bicycles.

CONTENTS

INTRODUCTION

Yes, there have been plenty of other books about so-called man skills, but they've all been a bit too bow-tie and light-a-barbecue for my liking.

This, I hope, is different. There are only nine topics, but they are not, as far as I can discern, covered anywhere else. That makes this book indispensable in a sea of duplicated 'how to' manuals; the one tin of fortifying Spam in the post-apocalyptic corner shop of putrefying groceries.

The chances that you will ever meet
with the circumstances outlined here
are, frankly, very remote. But you're
still better off knowing this stuff than
not knowing it. One day, there may
well be an A330 Airbus wandering
pilotlessly over the Atlantic, and
someone will have to land it.

Life is a lottery, and maybe, just
maybe, it could be you. But only
if you've read this.

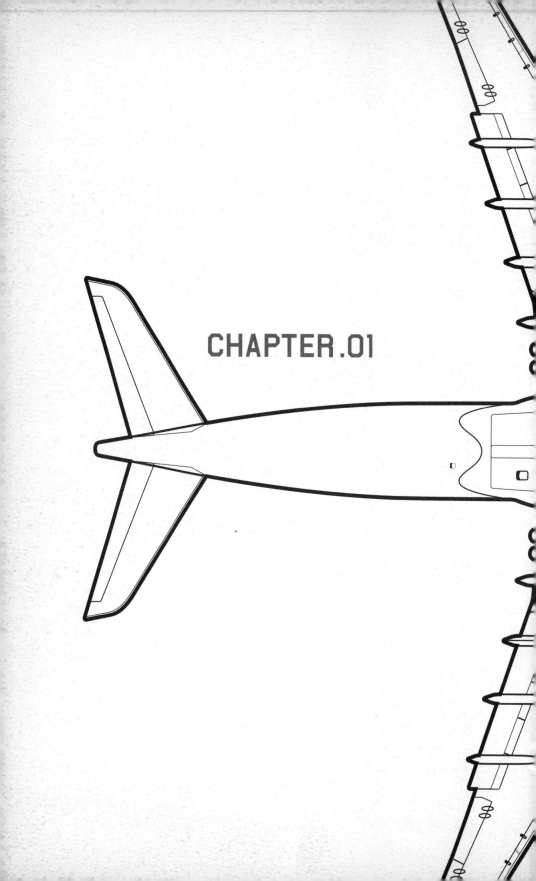

CHAPTER.01

HOW TO LAND AN

A330
AIRBUS

IN AN EMERGENCY

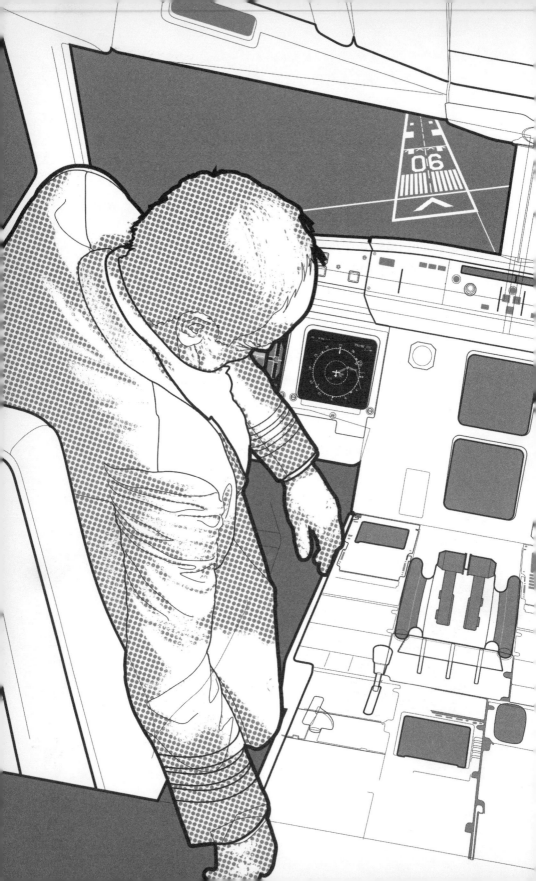

This is one of the most compelling hero fantasies the world has to offer. The crew has been murdered or laid out by manky prawns from the in-flight meal, and the aircraft is at 38,000 feet, pilotless. It can stay there until the fuel runs out and it falls to earth, or you can seize the controls from the limp grasp of the expired captain and bring it in to rapturous acclaim and probably a refund on the price of your ticket.

And why wouldn't you? The airliner crisis is a unique proposition, because its audience of potential victims is a completely captive one. You can wait for a ship to sink and possibly swim to safety; you can turn your back on the drowning man or the blazing apartment block; and you can hide in the stationery cupboard during the late-night office petty cash heist and never have to admit to having been there.

But there's no way out of the runaway aeroplane. So even though, ostensibly, you'll be saving the lives of everyone on board, in reality, you'll only be saving your own skin. The rest of the world, however, will not see it that way.

He should have known never to have the vegetarian option.

'Proclaimed the saviour of all women and children'

14

Because the other enduring truism of airline dramas is that everyone involved is always a hero. If a seasoned captain of twenty years' experience, fully versed in emergency procedures and regularly practised in discharging them, so much as lands an aircraft with a slightly bald nose wheel tyre, he will be proclaimed the saviour of all women and children. Even before the investigation into a forced landing or crash has begun, the face of the bloke who was in the hot seat at the moment of impact will be emblazoned across the front of the *Daily Mirror* along with citations from air traffic controllers and survivors confirming how calm he remained. And if, later on, it emerges that he simply made a bit of a cock-up, everyone will be too polite to mention it. This is why you never see newspaper headlines like:

DAFT BUGGER CAPTAIN
SHUT DOWN REMAINING GOOD ENGINE

Or

'I FORGOT',
ADMITS PILOT IN WHEELS-UP
RUNWAY INFERNO TRAGEDY

Headlines you never see. You can only come out of this well.

Urban Arts
Mike Garland
Talks Graffiti / PAGE 33

Politics
The Bobby Birchall
Expose / PAGE 40

THE DAILY TELEGRAM

Friday, June, 4, 2010   www.BRITAINS BEST SELLER.com   No. 47,545   70p

'I forgot', admits pilot

Sed ut perspiciatis unde omnis iste natus error sit voluptatem accusantium doloremque laudantium, totam rem aperiam.

Neque porro quisquam est, qui dolorem ipsum quia dolor sit amet, consectetur, adipisci velit, sed quia non numquam eius modi tempora incidunt ut labore et dolore magnam aliquam quaerat voluptatem.

Ut enim ad minima veniam, quis nostrum exercitationem ullam corporis suscipit laboriosam, nisi ut aliquid ex ea commodi consequatur?

error sit voluptatem accusantium doloremque laudantium, totam rem aperiam, eaque ipsa quae ab illo inventore veritatis et quasi architecto beatae vitae dicta sunt explicabo. Nemo enim ipsam voluptatem quia voluptas sit aspernatur aut odit aut fugit, sed quia consequuntur magni dolores eos qui ratione voluptatem sequi nesciunt. Neque porro quisquam est, qui dolorem ipsum quia dolor sit amet, consectetur, adipisci velit, sed quia non numquam eius modi tempora incidunt ut labore et dolore magnam aliquam quaerat voluptatem. Ut enim ad minima veniam, quis nostrum exercitationem ullam corporis suscipit laboriosam, nisi ut aliquid ex ea commodi consequatur? Quis autem vel eum iure reprehenderit qui in ea voluptate velit esse quam nihil molestiae consequatur, vel illum qui dolorem eum fugiat quo voluptas nulla pariatur?"

voluptatem sequi nesciunt. Neque porro quisquam est, qui dolorem ipsum quia dolor sit amet, consectetur, adipisci velit, sed quia non numquam eius modi tempora incidunt ut labore et dolore magnam aliquam quaerat voluptatem. Ut enim ad minima veniam, quis nostrum exercitationem ullam corporis suscipit laboriosam, nisi ut aliquid ex ea commodi consequatur?

Sed ut perspiciatis unde omnis iste natus error sit voluptatem accusantium doloremque laudantium, totam rem aperiam.

Neque porro quisquam est, qui dolorem ipsum quia dolor sit amet, consectetur, adipisci velit, sed quia non numquam eius modi tempora incidunt ut labore et dolore magnam aliquam quaerat voluptatem. Ut enim ad minima veniam, quis nostrum exercitationem ullam corporis suscipit laboriosam, nisi ut aliquid ex ea commodi consequatur?

TELEGRAM

Captain facing high-court prosecution

Full editorial comment
Page 12

Sed ut perspiciatis unde omnis iste natus error sit voluptatem accusantium doloremque laudantium, totam rem aperiam, eaque ipsa quae ab illo inventore veritatis et quasi architecto beatae vitae dicta sunt explicabo. Nemo enim ipsam voluptatem quia voluptas sit aspernatur aut odit aut fugit, sed quia consequuntur magni dolores eos qui ratione voluptatem sequi nesciunt. Neque porro quisquam est, qui dolorem ipsum quia dolor sit amet, consectetur, adipisci velit, sed quia non numquam eius modi tempora incidunt ut labore et dolore magnam aliquam quaerat voluptatem. Ut enim ad minima veniam, quis nostrum exercitationem ullam corporis suscipit laboriosam, nisi ut aliquid ex ea commodi consequatur?

Sed ut perspiciatis unde omnis iste natus error sit voluptatem accusantium doloremque laudantium, totam rem aperiam, eaque ipsa quae ab illo inventore veritatis et quasi architecto beatae vitae dicta sunt explicabo. Nemo enim ipsam voluptatem quia voluptas sit aspernatur aut odit aut fugit, sed quia consequuntur magni dolores eos qui ratione voluptatem sequi nesciunt.

Disgraced
Captain leaves court yesterday

Sed ut perspiciatis unde omnis iste natus error sit voluptatem accusantium doloremque laudantium, totam rem aperiam, eaque ipsa quae ab illo inventore veritatis et quasi architecto beatae vitae dicta sunt explicabo. Nemo enim ipsam voluptatem quia voluptas sit aspernatur aut odit aut fugit, sed quia consequuntur magni dolores eos qui ratione voluptatem sequi nesciunt. Neque porro quisquam est, qui dolorem ipsum quia dolor sit amet, consectetur, adipisci velit, sed quia non numquam eius modi tempora incidunt ut labore et dolore magnam aliquam quaerat voluptatem. Ut enim ad minima veniam, quis nostrum exercitationem ullam corporis suscipit laboriosam, nisi ut aliquid ex ea commodi consequatur?

voluptatem sequi nesciunt. Neque porro quisquam est, qui dolorem ipsum quia dolor sit amet, consectetur, adipisci velit, sed quia non numquam eius modi tempora incidunt ut labore et dolore magnam aliquam quaerat voluptatem. Ut enim ad minima veniam, quis nostrum exercitationem ullam corporis suscipit laboriosam, nisi ut aliquid ex ea commodi consequatur?

Sed ut perspiciatis unde omnis iste natus error sit voluptatem accusantium doloremque laudantium, totam rem aperiam.

Neque porro quisquam est, qui dolorem ipsum quia dolor sit amet, consectetur, adipisci velit, sed quia non numquam eius modi tempora incidunt ut labore et dolore magnam aliquam quaerat voluptatem.

A good day to bury £10bn of airline losses

By Rachel Garland
Reporter 1

Sed ut perspiciatis unde omnis iste natus error sit voluptatem accusantium doloremque laudantium, totam rem aperiam, eaque ipsa quae ab illo inventore veritatis et quasi architecto beatae vitae dicta sunt explicabo. Nemo enim ipsam voluptatem quia voluptas

Quis autem vel eum iure reprehenderit qui in ea voluptate velit esse quam nihil molestiae consequatur, vel illum qui dolorem eum fugiat quo voluptas nulla pariatur?"

voluptatem sequi nesciunt. Neque porro quisquam est, qui dolorem ipsum quia dolor sit amet, consectetur, adipisci velit, sed quia non numquam eius modi tempora incidunt ut labore et dolore magnam aliquam quaerat voluptatem.

Quis autem vel eum iure reprehenderit qui in ea voluptate velit esse quam nihil molestiae consequatur, vel illum qui dolorem eum fugiat quo voluptas nulla pariatur?"

voluptatem sequi nesciunt. Neque porro quisquam est, qui dolorem ipsum quia dolor sit amet, consectetur, adipisci velit, sed quia non numquam eius modi tempora incidunt ut labore et dolore magnam aliquam quaerat voluptatem.

'Hammering on the window and screaming for your mother'

This sort of revelation is reserved for the turgid accident reports in the backs of magazines such as *Flight International*, and only other pilots read that rubbish.

So you're not going to come out of this one badly. If you do manage to land the aeroplane successfully, or even only half successfully, you will probably be commemorated in stone on that spare plinth in Trafalgar Square, and will save all the money that had otherwise been earmarked for beer over the rest of your life. Even if you fly it at 300 knots into the local hospital, the press will still feel obliged to point out how you at least had a go and stayed at your post to the bitter end. Although the transcripts of black box flight recorders are invariably published, the Air Accidents Investigation Board usually edits out blasphemy and incomprehensible mumblings, and it's reasonable to assume that they would see no benefit to the world in revealing that you ended up babbering your pants, hammering on the window and screaming for your mother. But don't do it anyway, just to be on the safe side.

And let's be honest here. In truth, the chances of the scenario outlined in paragraph one ever developing are extremely unlikely. Both pilots would have to be completely incapacitated in some way or simultaneously overtaken by suicidal religious zeal, and while one or the other can

In a real emergency, it is not actually necessary to dress up.

18

sometimes fall victim to this sort of thing, it's unlikely that both will. That, in fact, is why there are two of them.

And then there's this to consider. Let's assume you are an accountant, with no experience whatsoever of flying aeroplanes. The odds that, out of the 300 or so people on board, you will be the best qualified to take control are pretty slim. Other airline pilots are often travelling on commercial flights. Cabin crew sometimes have an interest in flying and a good working knowledge of the aircraft's controls. There's a reasonable statistical chance that somewhere amongst the passengers there will be a former RAF Bomber Command pilot, a holder of a private pilot's licence, an aircraft maintenance engineer or even just an enthusiast of computer-based flight simulators. If you're unlucky, you might even be sitting next to one of them. All of these people are a better bet than you.

But having said that, on 11 September 2001 passengers aboard United Airlines flight 93 were forced down a circumstantial avenue in which they had no choice but to attempt to wrest control of the aircraft from its hijackers. And it's always possible that you bought a cheap ticket from a bucket shop, and now find yourself in the only spare seat on a charter flight full of nuns. In which case it's time to seize the moment, along with something called the 'joystick'.

Deposit the dead pilot in the cheap seats near the lavatories.

First, though, make your way to the flight deck, and discover that the door leading to it is locked. This has been a requirement since 9/11, in an attempt to prevent unauthorised access by terrorists, and even in the midst of this unfolding melodrama it is worth pausing for a second to reflect on the deep irony of it all. A cabin attendant should be able to unlock it for you.

The illustration overleaf shows how the cockpit of the A330 will look once you have heaved the helpless carcasses of the captain and first officer out of their seats, taking care not to snag any important-looking levers on their clothing. This would have presented a far more terrifying prospect not so long ago, in the era when the instrument panel of a commercial airliner was a mass of incomprehensible analogue dials. But on the A330, as on almost all modern airliners, these have largely been usurped by a mere handful of incomprehensible computer screens (Fig. 1, overleaf).

Fortunately, and as with the fascias of most large Mercedes Benz cars, most of it is completely useless to you. Fig. 2

shows the same view with all but the most vital controls and instruments ghosted out. All those knobs and buttons above the windscreen control such trivialities as the cabin temperature, the windscreen wipers and the seat-belt warning signs. Similarly, the small computer mounted horizontally on what would be the centre console if this were a VW Golf gives advice on such inconsequentialities as engine maintenance intervals. None of this is very pressing at the moment, and could become completely academic if the aeroplane ends up at the bottom of the Irish Sea. Forget them (Fig. 2, p. 24).

For the moment, relax. Assuming the aircraft is in the cruise, the autopilot will almost certainly be engaged and you can take time to familiarise yourself with what pilots sometimes call 'the office'. Convention says that the captain of a fixed-wing aircraft sits on the left, and as the cruel mistress of fate has conspired with Melpomene, the muse of tragic drama, to cast you in this new and unrehearsed role, that is where you should sit.

Now you must make your emergency call to air traffic control, and for this you will need the aircraft's call sign, which will be displayed somewhere on the panel in front of you on a small plaque. Let's say we are aboard G-ABCD.[1]

---

1. The registration G-ABCD actually belonged to a now deregistered Avro Avian biplane of 1920s vintage, and no slur against this wonderful machine is intended.

A330 Flight Deck

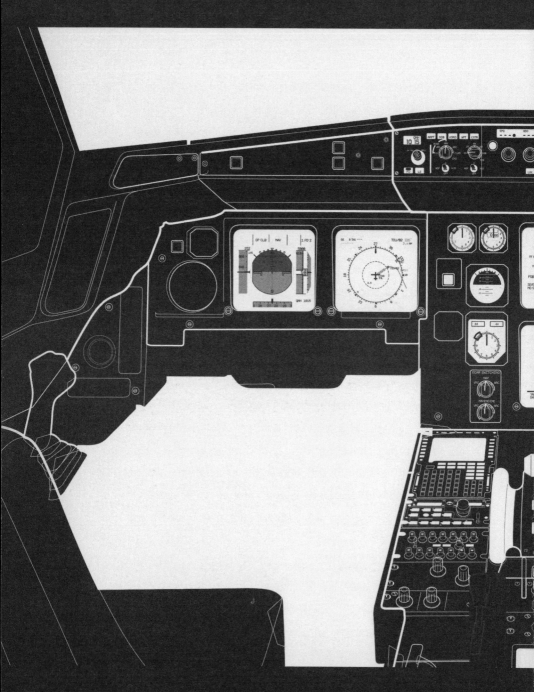

Fig. 1: What you will see on entering the flight deck.

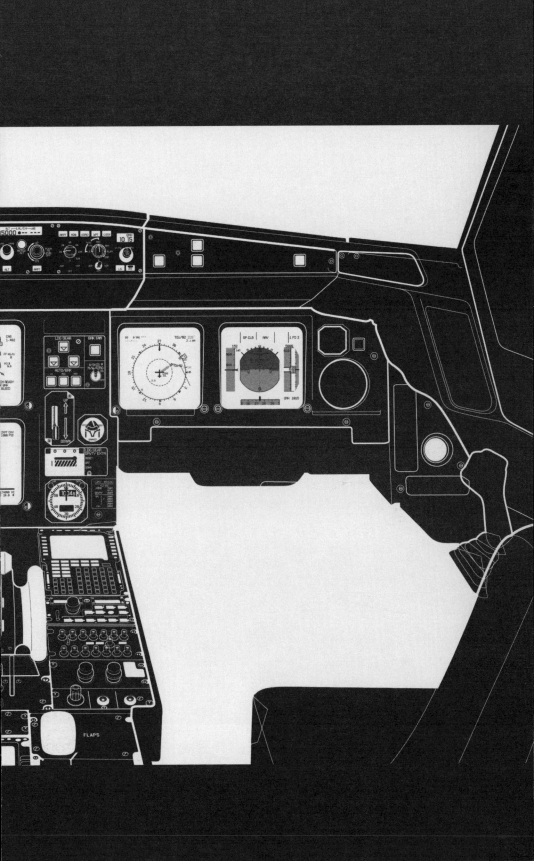

Fig. 2: What you actually need to worry about.

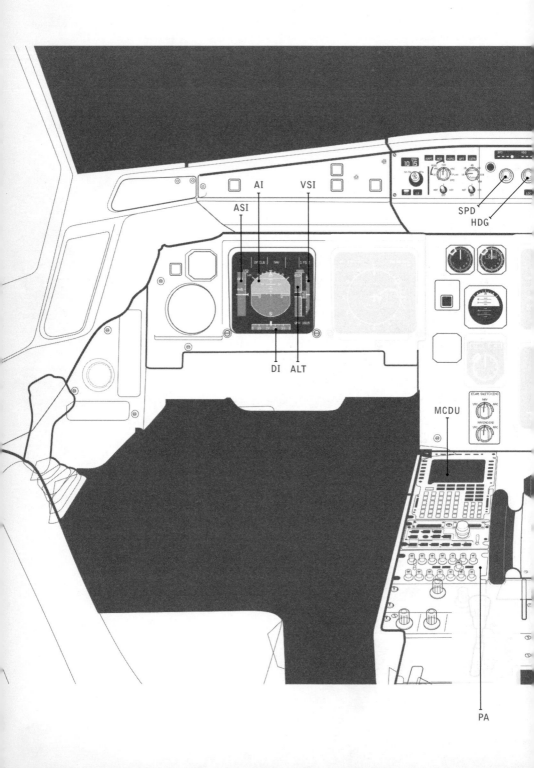

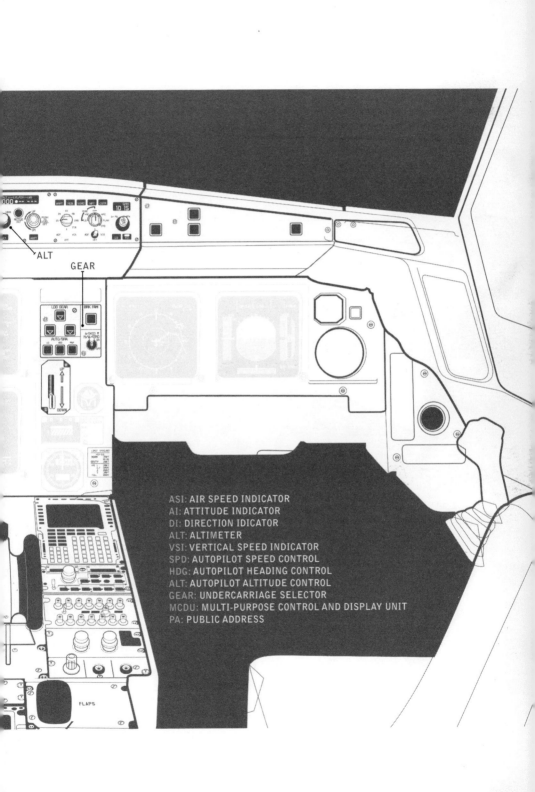

ALT

GEAR

ASI: AIR SPEED INDICATOR
AI: ATTITUDE INDICATOR
DI: DIRECTION IDICATOR
ALT: ALTIMETER
VSI: VERTICAL SPEED INDICATOR
SPD: AUTOPILOT SPEED CONTROL
HDG: AUTOPILOT HEADING CONTROL
ALT: AUTOPILOT ALTITUDE CONTROL
GEAR: UNDERCARRIAGE SELECTOR
MCDU: MULTI-PURPOSE CONTROL AND DISPLAY UNIT
PA: PUBLIC ADDRESS

FLAPS

Put on the headset and depress the PTT (Press To Talk) button on the joystick. A hideous, spike-infested pitfall awaits you here. The red button on top of the stick – the one that falls so readily under your thumb – is NOT the press-to-talk. It is the autopilot override, and will end your bid to be immortalised alongside Alcock and Brown very abruptly. The

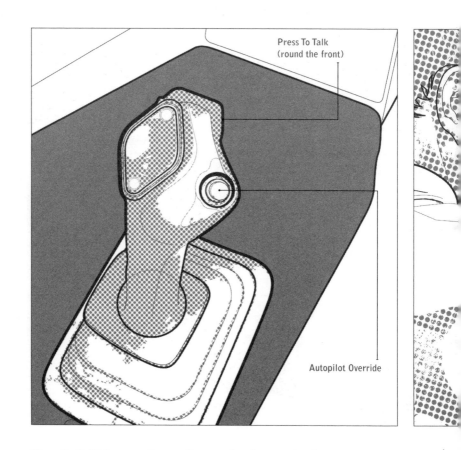

Fig. 3: Talking on the radio vs. losing control.

PTT is the trigger-like switch on the front of the joystick, where the gun button would be on a video game (Fig. 3).

Should you press the red button by mistake, immediately press AP1 (Fig. 4) and the autopilot will revert to the flight plan that was entered in the computer at take-off.

Fig. 4: Reinstating the autopilot, your best friend.

Calm, level, clipped, clear, unhurried'

Now, and in a voice that is calm, level, clipped, clear, unhurried, tinged with icy resolve and everything else you will want them to write about you in the following day's tabloids, say something like:

'Mayday, mayday, mayday. Golf Alfa Bravo Charlie Delta. Pilot and first officer disabled. I am a passenger, I have taken control and I await your instructions.'

The international language of air traffic control is English, so even over the Greek islands whoever is listening will be shaken from his or her diurnal torpor by the textbook professionalism of your transmission. It's such a shame that person is unlikely to be a pilot 'current on type' for the A330.

So while the controller desperately rings around in search of someone who can help you over the radio, you may as well continue to relax. Remember – the autopilot is still on, and the autopilot is your best friend. At the very least, it is a much better pilot than you are. You could even press the PA button (Fig. 5), talk to the passengers and advise them of the outside air temperature. Don't worry about getting the temperature exactly right – minus 32 will do – as they don't actually care, but the calming effect of familiar and meaningless pilot babble will be welcomed in the cheap seats.

Fig. 5: Why not share a reassuring and light-hearted observation with your terrified passengers?

Take a moment to familiarise yourself with the small screen directly ahead of you. It shows, from left to right, the air speed indicator (how fast you're going), the attitude indicator (or artificial horizon), the altimeter (how high you are) and the vertical speed indicator (how quickly you're climbing or descending). Along the bottom is the direction indicator (your compass heading). Useful operational parameters are as follows:

Air speed indicator (ASI): keep the speed between the two red 'bugs' at the top and bottom of the scale. Above the top one and the aircraft could fall apart; below the bottom one and it will stall and fall out of the sky, in accordance with Newton. Speeds are in knots.

Attitude indicator (AI): the blue part should remain roughly at the top and the black bit at the bottom, with the division between the two fairly close to the middle of the display. If it appears the other way up, you can skip the bit about lowering the undercarriage.

Altimeter (Alt): height is good, as it buys you time. But it can also easily translate into excess speed, so...

Vertical speed indicator (VSI): avoid climbs and descents of more than 2000ft per minute.

Direction indicator (DI): compass headings are expressed
with the last digit omitted, so 27 is actually 270 degrees,
i.e., west.

The next thing you will probably have to do is retune the
radio, possibly to another air traffic control station, possibly
even to another Airbus in flight, but most likely to the
international distress frequency of 121.50. This will be
expressed by the controller as 'one two one decimal five zero'.
On the right-hand side of the radio module is a large knob of
two different diameters. The lower, fatter portion alters the
numbers to the left of the decimal point, the slimmer portion,
those numbers to the right. Your new frequency will appear
on the right of the digital display, in 'standby'. Once you are
happy with it, press the little button and it will be transferred
to the 'active' side on the left (Fig. 6 overleaf).

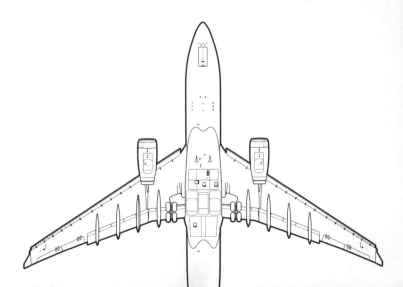

You are now ready to fly the Airbus to an airport, under instruction from the controller, using the autopilot. There are just three knobs to worry about here, and they control airspeed, heading and altitude (Fig. 7).

Fig. 6: Tuning the radio. New frequencies appear in 'standby'.

Airbus Industries' flawless control logic says that when the knobs are pulled out, control rests with the pilot. When they are pushed in, it rests with the pre-programmed flight computer. Therefore, pull them out when instructed to make inputs, otherwise the aircraft will blithely continue to head where it was already going, which could be Hong Kong.

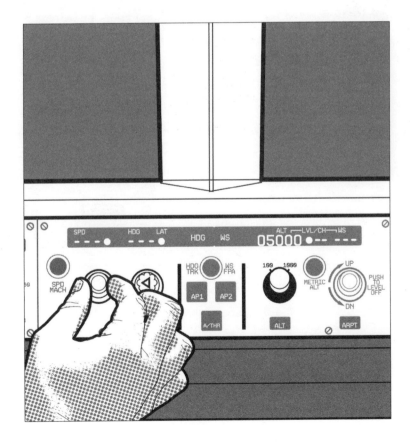

Fig. 7: Autopilot controls. Pull knob to make changes.

Simply twirl the knobs until the values given by the controller appear on the digital display. By this means you will be able to fly the aeroplane to an airport with no more difficulty than you would have in setting the timer on a microwave oven. But don't tell anyone.

If air traffic control has any sense – and these people are generally selected for their intelligence and cool-headedness – they will have directed you to an airport that will allow you to use the Airbus's Instrument Landing System (or ILS). If you have been vectored to a remote runway on a disused airbase where you have no choice but to land the aeroplane manually, you may as well forget it, because, as the A330 captain consulted in the preparation of this work put it, 'Everyone will be killed.' There will be nothing for it but to say something memorable on the radio. Pithy reflections about your love for the family or your regret at having failed everyone should get you the front page.

As you make your way on autopilot to the airport, you will have to programme the ILS in the cockpit using the Multi-purpose Control and Display Unit, or MCDU, or 'McDoo' in the chummy lexicon of real pilots. This is near your right knee (Fig. 8).

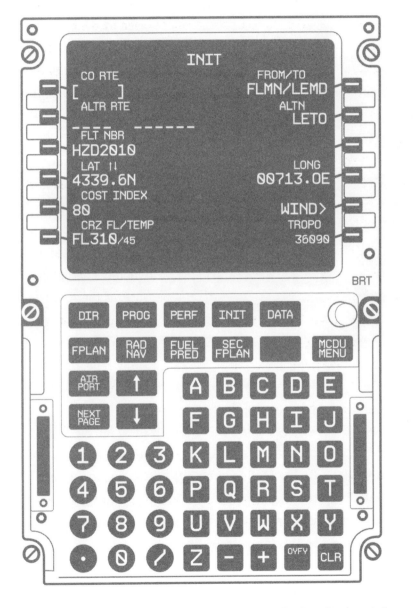

Fig. 8: The MCDU. Not as complicated as it looks. Fortunately.

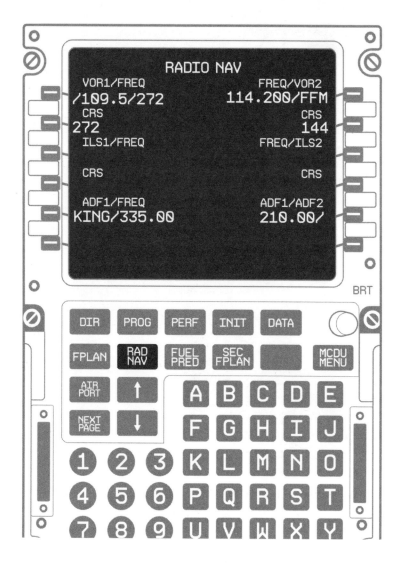

Control will give you a frequency and heading for the ILS of the airport; in the case of London Heathrow, it will be 109.5/272. On the McDoo, press the button marked RAD/NAV. Enter the frequency and heading with the keypad and, when they appear on the screen, press the little button alongside. The ILS is now programmed but not yet active (Fig. 9).

Fig. 9: Programming the Instrument Landing System.

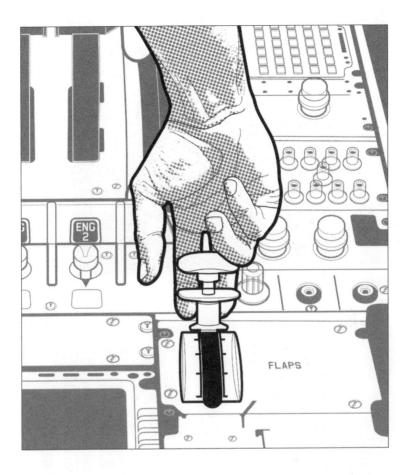

By now, control will have instructed you to descend using the autopilot, and you will be nearing 3000 feet. It is time to slow the Airbus down for the final approach. Using the speed knob on the autopilot, gently wind the airspeed down until it is about 10 knots above the lower red 'bug' on the ASI. Now select the first stage of flap, using the conveniently flap-shaped lever (Fig. 10).

With the wings now generating more lift, that lower bug on the ASI will move to a lower speed. Repeat the above process for the second stage of flap – slow to 10 knots above the bug, pull the lever.

Fig. 10: Lowering the flaps. Observe the ASI bug.

Next, control will direct you to intercept something called QDM, which is the heading to the runway. Again, this is a simple matter of twiddling the knobs on the autopilot. Once flying straight and level on the right heading, you can initiate the ILS you programmed earlier. Just press the button marked APPR (for 'approach') on the autopilot and the Airbus will make its own way to the runway. Even the throttles will be controlled automatically.

But there is still much work for you to do before attaining glory. Lower the undercarriage using the lever over on the first officer's side (Fig. 11).

Three green lights on the display above will confirm that it is down and locked. Next, and after reducing the airspeed to around 15 knots above the lower bug, deploy the final two stages of flap.

The aircraft will seem to you to be travelling absurdly slowly towards the runway, which should now be visible. Resist the urge to push the throttles open or pull back on the joystick. The automatic controls have been conceived and engineered by people who know so much more than you about the performance of the aircraft that to doubt them would be an insult. You will also be remembered by history as yet

Fig. 11: Lower the undercarriage. A small lever does a very big job, but that's no excuse for forgetting.

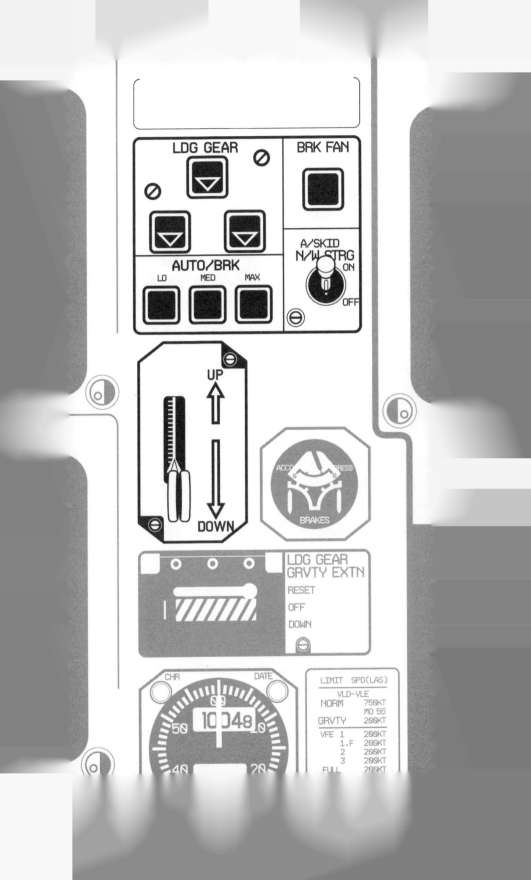

another bloke who thought he knew better, and you don't. Leave everything alone and sit on your hands.

At the runway threshold, the nose will also seem to be pointing too far down. Again, do not interfere. It will 'flare' automatically; that is, lift its nose to increase lift just before touchdown and lower the rate of descent. As soon as the main wheels make contact with the runway, pull the two throttles right back until they will go no further, the 'idle' position. The end of the runway will tilt into view and the nose wheel will touch down.

All that remains is to stop. Press with your toes on the rudder pedals to work the wheel brakes. At the same time, lift the small levers on the back of the throttles, which will allow them to move further backwards. This triggers reverse thrust from the engines. Once the aeroplane has slowed to a brisk trot return the throttles to idle and come to a halt using your feet.

Apply the parking brake, shut down the engines by lifting and twisting the knobs marked ENG 1 and ENG 2, press the PA button and say 'Cabin crew, doors to manual.' If you happen to have landed at Barcelona it is permissible to say 'Cabin crew, doors to Manuel.' It's an old joke, but the nuns probably haven't heard it and tensions will be so high in the cabin that you're more guaranteed of a laugh than the bride's father.

Now report to the control tower for a cup of tea and a truly enormous medal.

AUTHOR'S DISCLAIMER

This guide has been prepared only for use in absolute dire, buttock-clenching emergency. None of the advice given above has been sanctioned by Airbus or any of its associates. Do not attempt to fly the A330 Airbus on a recreational basis, or use one for joyriding in a hoodie. **The A330 Airbus is not a toy.**

INCLUDES DISCLAIMER!

BRITISH MAYDAYS

You may feel your air miles account swelling enormously.

TER TWO

BUTLINS
HOLIDAY CAMP

Approved 2?
Scale 05.25m

HOW TO

from **BUT**

'This migration of holidaymakers to the sea... is as typical of European culture as were the bread and circuses of ancient Rome'

– JAR Pimlott, *The Englishman's Holiday*, 1947

If this bloke Pimlott had done his research properly, he would have discovered that the Englishman's holiday of which he spoke so blithely was a hard-won privilege that took half a millennium to secure for the common man.

Prior to the sixteenth century, the very notion that sons of toil should be allowed any relief from their tireless labour at the forge or from behind the gleaming teak handle of the God-sped plough, oiled and nourished as it was through the sweat of barely rewarded endeavour, was preposterous. Time off on Sunday for singing hymns around the wheezing harmonium was about as good as it got. The sickie hadn't yet been invented.

The possible exception, but only for a fortunate few, was the religious pilgrimage. This is why Chaucer's *Canterbury Tales* was considered such a rollicking good read. To most people,

lurid yarns of farting
and intercourse'

46

HOW TO ESCAPE FROM BUTLINS

the idea of 'sondry folk' bunking off to visit a shrine, swapping lurid yarns of farting and intercourse as they go, would have seemed as fantastical as *Star Trek*.

For the wealthy, the landed and the indulged things were different, of course. They had been swanning around Italy and France for generations, and by the time of Victoria the 'grand tour' of Europe was an accepted part of the formation of good character in the upper-class young. The proles, however, were not generally spared the job of propping up the empire. In Dickens' *A Christmas Carol*, Bob Cratchit the clerk is chided for wanting the *whole* of Christmas day off, the ungrateful peasant.

The working classes' ultimate descent into idleness was kick-started with the Bank Holidays Act of 1871, which decreed that trading would not be allowed on significant days in the Christian calendar, thus allowing the plebs to kick their heels in the park.[1]

But final and complete liberation would have to wait for the Annual Holiday Bill of 1936. This seminal piece of legislation proposed not only that working people should be granted at least six consecutive work-free days for the purposes of taking a restorative holiday, but that they should *continue to be paid while on it.* As a result of this, we ended up with Butlins.

1. New Year's Day did not become an official Bank Holiday until 1974.

Billy (later Sir Billiam) Butlin (1899–1980) founded his first holiday camp at Skegness, in 1936, on a simple premise: 'A week's holiday for a week's pay' (typically 35 bob[2] at the time). The money you were earning for doing, frankly, sod-all should be given to him, and in return he'd give you a grand time at the seaside, everything thrown in, and all in one place so the ruling classes would know where you were.

Some of the temptations that Butlin laid in front of the first generation of common holidaymakers read today more like the specification for an open prison: three square meals a day,

2. That's £1.75 in the Roman Catholic money.

BUTLIN'S HOLIDAY CAMP
CHEEKY-WEEK-AWAY
IT'S QUICKER BY RAIL
ILLUSTRATED BOOKLET FREE FROM R. P. BUTLIN'S PUBLICITY DEPARTMENT, SKEGNESS, OR ANY L·N·E·R OFFICE OR AGENCY

Billy Butlin (middle).

for example, and the electric light and running water in every chalet! But these things were not givens in the dreary B&B-based holiday culture of 1930s Britain, and still aren't, come to think of it.

Billy Butlin, the man who had introduced dodgems to the UK in 1923, was in fact a visionary and a philanthropist. His nine eventual camps saved countless thousands from blowing a week's cash on Woodbines, mild and dog-racing, or catching consumption because they were locked out of a slum guest house in Southend during the freezing British August nights. The capacity of his Skegness site grew from 500 to 1200 after just one season, and would eventually house close to 10,000 if you include the static caravan park. It might all seem a bit 'Take my wife – please' in

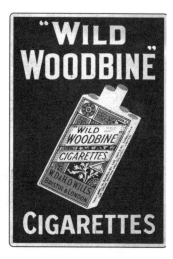

this day and age but the talent crucible that is the Redcoats tradition has produced some of the country's greatest names – Cliff Richard and Jimmy Tarbuck.

So any suggestion that Butlins is just a thinly disguised concentration camp is scurrilous, ill-informed and a grave insult to its founder. Yes, there are some obvious parallels. Butlins Skegness is effectively a compound, the original accommodation is basic and regimented, there are communal areas for the purposes of feeding the inmates and distracting them, through 'entertainment', from fomenting dissidence, and the whole is managed and patrolled by uniformed staff. It must be acknowledged that very little was required to convert it to a naval base during World War II.

But 'concentration camp' can be defined as a compound for the indiscriminate detainment of people on the basis of ethnicity, nationality, beliefs or activity, so Butlins doesn't qualify, unless we regard people who want to holiday in Britain as dangerous lunatics.

Comparison between the Butlins take on holiday nirvana and that envisaged in Germany at the same time, during the rise of the Reich, is quite revealing. Prora, the 1936 resort on Rügen Island, was a similar but much more ambitious idea, designed to house up to 20,000 members of the *Deutsche Arbeitsfront*, or German Workers' Front, in massive, soulless accommodation blocks, rather than small ones. It was part of the Nazis' *Kraft Durch Freude* or 'strength through joy' programme, through which your loyal worker would achieve spiritual completeness and unquestioning loyalty through morning exercise, bunting and community singing. We had mother-in-law jokes.

PRORA (RÜGEN)

Am 4.5.1945 erreicht die Rote Armee Rügen - hier beginnt die "rote" Geschich

Unusually for a German project, Prora was never actually finished, and ended up as a ruin in the Eastern Bloc. Butlins Skegness went on to feature Britain's first monorail and is vibrant to this day. Under the Nazis, the holiday camp would soon give way to the true concentration camp, in which millions would be murdered. Butlins Skegness, although at a glance it might look similar, was the birthplace of Ringo Starr's career, which seems like a fairly mild crime against humanity by comparison. The gates of Nazi camps were infamously emblazoned with the legend *Arbeit Macht Frei* – work makes you free. Under National Socialism, work generally made you dead, but in happy Britain it really did set you free. You worked hard, you got a week off on full pay, and you could have as much putting, ping-pong and Bernard Manning as you wanted. So let's not knock Butlins.

However, Butlin did make one serious mistake. Given the clouds of war that were gathering in the mid-1930s, and Britain's naked unpreparedness for resisting invasion, it was

1930s Germany was never an especially popular holiday destination with the British. It's not entirely clear why.

faintly irresponsible to provide potential occupying forces with something so conveniently located, that could be used as an internment camp. Since Butlins Skegness still exists, and our ability to resist invasion is once again woefully diminished by the deployment of our troops overseas, there is still a danger that as an undesirable element – a reader of the *Daily Telegraph*, for example – you could be banged up in Skeggy for a lot longer than a week, and without any pay at all.

In which case, it's worth knowing how to get out.

Without question, the most efficient way to liberate a large number of the camp's potential 10,000 detainees in one go is through a tunnel. Romantic notions of staining prison garb with tomato sauce from a tomato-shaped dispenser (to pass yourself off as a Redcoat) or perming your hair in order to sneak out unnoticed with a departing '80s tribute band will free only one or two people at a time and, once used, cannot hope to be used successfully again.

Overground escape attempts should, in fact, be dismissed entirely, except perhaps as part of an orchestrated programme of diversionary tactics. It is quite likely that the new Kommandants of Butlitz will set up a series of interlocking

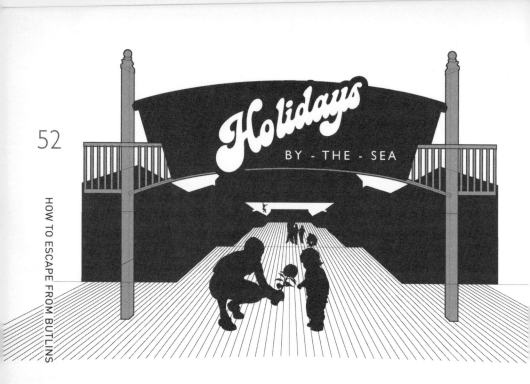

perimeter defences similar to those used by the GDR around the Berlin Wall, perhaps turning the A52 into a brightly floodlit 'death strip' where guards would be permitted to fire at will on escapees.

A well-engineered tunnel could free prisoners from Butlins at
such an astonishing rate that the entire prison population could
make a 'home run' over the course of a single night.

Tunnelling has been a favoured method of escape pretty much
since prisons were created. As recently as 2003 more than
eighty prisoners dug their way out of Brazil's Silvio Porto prison,
inspired perhaps by the efforts of one hundred of their kind in
2001, who successfully bored their way out of the high-security
prison at Carandiru. One of these, Moises Teixeira da Silva, later
went on to tunnel his way seventy-eight metres from a rented
house and into a bank, where he netted $67.8 million. So
tunnelling out of Butlins also offers the opportunity to acquire a
useful life skill in the way that hiding in a laundry bag doesn't.

During the cold war, a number of successful escape tunnels
were dug between East and West Berlin, notably the one in the
basement of 60 Westerstrasse, through which twenty-nine fled
before it was discovered. Another was started from a graveyard,
so one of a group of 'mourners' could simply drop to freedom
and be reincarnated in the West.

But undoubtedly the most famous tunnel escape in history was
that made by the aircrew POWs of Stalag Luft III during the spring
of 1944, as celebrated in the film *The Great Escape* whenever

*Transforming Butlins from a holiday camp into a gulag would be a challenge
many a 1960s town planner would embrace with delight.*

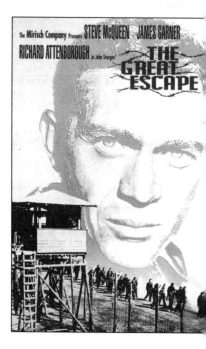

the cricket is rained off. Seventy-six men made it through the 115-metre tunnel 'Harry', although all but three were recaptured.

The enduring popularity of *The Great Escape*, along with *The Wooden Horse* and the original BBC *Colditz* series, has left your prospective modern British PoW fairly well informed on matters of tunnelling. Or has it? We all know it has to start under something like a stove, that you get rid of soil on the vegetable patch via bags hidden in your trousers, that you should always say '*danke*' and not 'thanks' to avoid recapture, and so on. But what is never made fully clear is just what a gigantic feat of ad-hoc civil engineering tunnelling out of a prison camp actually is.

The three tunnels dug in Stalag Luft III (two abortive, one completed) produced 140 cubic metres of 'spoil' – around 200 tonnes – that had to be hidden. The project consumed 4000 bed boards, 90 double bunk beds, 635 mattresses, 1400 powdered milk tins, 3400 improvised trowels and 300 metres of electric cable. All this had to be removed from under the noses of the goons without arousing suspicion.

Occupying powers will have reckoned without the inspirational teachings of Steve McQueen.

There is also a geometric conundrum to be overcome in any hand-tunnelling scheme. The bigger the size of the bore, the more spoil has to be removed and disposed of. Increasing the diameter of a circular bore from 1m to 1.5m increases the volume of spoil by 125 per cent. It should also be remembered that a given volume of compacted earth expands by up to 50 per cent when it is removed and broken up, a phenomenon known as 'swell'. At the same time, if the tunnel is too small it limits the size of the tools that can be used inside it, lengthening the dig time enormously. The Great Escapers settled on tunnels roughly two-foot square, but they took over a year of continuous work to dig.

Risks inherent in tunnelling without the benefit of a proper survey include being buried alive, suffocating through lack of oxygen and burrowing into an underground stream or sewer and being drowned.

On the plus side, Skegness is located on the Lincolnshire coast, which is one of the few areas of Britain underpinned by alluvium, rather than clay or solid rock. This is relatively easy to dig through. In fact, such is the rate of coastal erosion around Skegness that you could simply spend a couple of centuries playing crazy golf and wait for the whole camp to be washed away.

The tunnel
Careful study of aerial reconnaissance photographs suggests that the ideal route for a tunnel would be to start underneath the

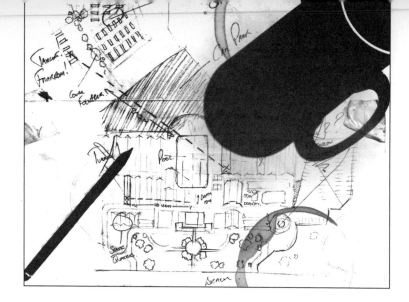

accommodation block to the north-east of the swimming pool and head roughly west to emerge in the nearby static caravan park.

This is pretty much the shortest route out of the compound, given the need to start somewhere secluded owing to the unlikelihood of getting away with the vaulting horse idea a second time. Passing beneath the presumably hefty foundations of the pool and the car park reduces the risk of subsidence, and the sound of tunnelling work will automatically be disguised by the noise coming from the pool area – splashing, giggling and loud exhortations to throw us the ball back mister.

The disadvantages include the need to first bore vertically to a depth of at least ten metres to avoid the risk of emptying the pool in the middle of a game of water polo or encountering unexpected utility pipes, which will generally be within five metres of the surface.

More to the point, even by this short route the tunnel works out at 240 metres long, or more than twice the length of 'Harry'. This would not only lead to the suspicious disappearance of every last bed in Butlins but also suggests a dig time, using traditional methods, of at least two years. Given that the 'undesirables' incarcerated in Butlins will probably be intellectuals, radical authors, media personalities and other limp-wristed fops rather than sturdy allied aircrew, we can probably double that.

Fortunately, help is at hand from our old escape allies.

The French connection

In the modern world, tunnelling has become a largely automated and mechanised affair. Of particular interest to us here is the technique of 'microboring'. This involves sending a small powered 'auger' underground along the proposed route of the tunnel, dragging behind it a steel cable. At the far end, this cable is attached to a small electric winch, and at the original end to a one-metre-diameter boring machine. The winch then simply drags the boring machine to its destination, cutting the tunnel as it goes and lining it in its wake with thick plastic piping. By this method it could be possible to dig a fully shored-up 240m tunnel in as little as ten days.

The French, for unknown reasons, are the world leaders in microboring. Coded postcards should be sent to major French civil engineering contractors requesting their assistance

The French

from outside the wire. In fact we may as well establish now that if any French tunnelling companies receive quaint retro postcards featuring a fat man and the slogan 'Skegness – it's so bracing', the real message is '*Gettez vous over to le static caravan parc avec le mechanisme du tunnelling, tout de suite, mes amis.*'

The main advantage of the microboring method is that the inmates are now required to dig only the vertical shaft at the camp end. This means less spoil to dispose of and less chance of being buried in a collapse. There remains the small matter of smuggling in the winch mechanism, but it seems likely that it could be dismantled and hidden among the equipment brought in by one of the pier-end magicians employed to keep the prisoners entertained, and then made to 'disappear' into the appropriate chalet.

The enormity of the task – the longest escape tunnel in camp history.

240 METRES

The Tunnel

The French party will also have to set up camp in the caravan park. Fortuitously, the boring machine and its equipment can be fitted inside one container, which is roughly the same size as a Butlins Gold-Plus static caravan. One of these can become their base, and the impression that something odd is going on inside can be readily explained on the basis that 'they're French'.

In return, the French will at last have an opportunity to redress the dreadful cod-accent atrocities perpetrated against their country during the *'Allo 'Allo* TV series.

The vertical shaft

Because of Skegness's soft ground, the chalet will almost certainly be built on a stout concrete plinth. This will have to be pierced using stolen or smuggled heavy hand tools, which in

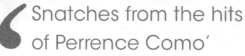
turn will create considerable noise. However, there are a number of established ways to disguise this.

Air hockey, recreational metalwork, a Black Sabbath tribute band or anything else that creates a regular and monotonous banging sound will perfectly cover up the regular strokes of pickaxes and lump hammers. But a better idea might be to ensure that there is a disaffected gum-chewing American amongst the prisoners. He can spend all day idly throwing a baseball against the side of the chalet, and keep lookout at the same time. This will also make it easier to sell the subsequent BBC dramatisation to a US TV network.

Once the concrete is pierced, the relatively easy spadework can commence, provided that the whole operation can be concealed from a spot chalet inspection within a minute. A tasteless floral rug secured to a sheet of plywood removed from the back of a wardrobe can be slid over the hole and a game of chess quickly set up. Lookouts posted around the camp can warn of approaching guards with a pre-arranged series of imitation birdcalls or snatches from the hits of Perrence Como. Or someone could simply open the door and say 'someone is coming'.

Note that at the bottom of the shaft a recess must be dug to accommodate the winch and to make space for the boring machine when it comes through from the French Resistance end.

This should be shored up with bed boards in the accepted *Colditz* fashion.

Once the shaft is dug one man will always be required to wait at the bottom for the arrival of the powered auger. In the event that *appel* is called during this time, he should be replaced in the line-up with a crude dummy or the life-size image of a faded radio personality cut from an old Butlins promotional poster and glued to a sheet of cardboard. This is a safe deception. The foreign occupying personnel will not recognise this person as a celebrity, just as no one at Butlins did.

Removal of spoil

If the vertical shaft is two metres in diameter to accommodate the forthcoming winch and ten metres deep, it will generate around forty-seven cubic metres of spoil, allowing for swell. This amounts to sixty-seven tonnes of loose earth. If dug at an achievable rate of half a metre a day, that means over three tonnes of earth will have to be disposed of every twenty-four hours.

A method that seems not to have been tried by British PoWs is that of digestion. It may be possible to mix the spoil with the slop being prepared by prison forced labour in the kitchens. If the 10,000 inmates of Butlins are being fed 1kg of meagre porridge each per day, then the spoil can be added as what the processed food business calls a 'bulking agent'. Even then, only around 30 per cent of any meal will be tunnel detritus. Resulting bowel disorders can be dismissed as 'holiday tummy'.

Alternatively, bogus tunnelling parties can be formed to explain the noise and to be caught disposing of what is actually spoil from the real tunnel. A further advantage of this approach is that all the fake tunnellers could be disguised as members of tribute bands, thus ensuring that when any real tribute bands arrive as part of the entertainments programme, they will be immediately banged up in the cooler before they've had a chance to perform 'Stairway to Heaven'.

Winching

The French, having already studied copies of this book dropped by night near Calais from a Westland Lysander, will know in which direction to send their initial boring auger. Once it arrives at the bottom of the shaft, the cable it has brought along will need to be attached to the winch smuggled in by the magician.

The French party will need to be able to indicate when they are ready for winching to begin. This may again be possible with coded postcards or messages concealed inside tins of boot polish in Red Cross parcels, but as they're only over the road they may just be able to shout. As before, this can be explained as part of being French.

The problem now is that operating the winch to draw the full-size boring machine along will demand a hefty three-phase mains electricity supply. This will require some creative wiring by the inmates, and will probably produce a noticeable flickering of lights around the camp and a possible erroneous and unfair 'tilt' warning on pinball machines.

Tribute bands may once more be the key to disguising escape activity. If the winch is operated during a performance by Van Halearen't or Nearvana, the impression that everything is getting darker will be attributed to low spirits rather than electrical malfunction.

Boring

There is little for the inmates to do during the boring process other than ensure continuous operation of the winch. Once the boring machine emerges in the camp's vertical shaft, the Frenchmen will have to know to turn it off. Since it has just presented you with a perfectly cut and plastic-lined route to their caravan, this is a simple matter of shouting *arret!* along its satisfyingly echoic length.

The escape

Before any mass breakout is attempted, one man should crawl through the completed tunnel in the role of a canary, to ensure that there is sufficient oxygen supply. If he dies, bellows will have to be fashioned out of bedding materials and wood (see *The Great Escape*). Alternatively, one of Butlins' former stand-up acts could be re-employed as a windbag.

This exercise will also reveal that it takes a man at least fifteen minutes to crawl along a one-metre-diameter 240m-long

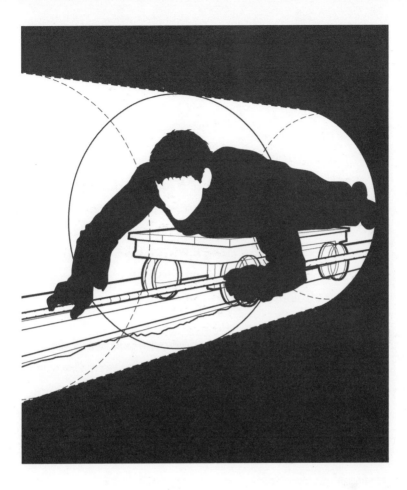

tunnel. Even if one prisoner enters the tunnel every minute, risking an encounter with the previous man's flatulence and further heightening the risk of suffocation, it would take seven whole days to free the entire camp population, during which time *appel* would almost certainly be called and the plan discovered.

It would make sense to construct some sort of underground railway, again in the style of the Great Escapers, and use the camp winch and something similar at the French end to speed everyone through.

Traditionally, this would involve laying some crude wooden rails hewn from whatever bits of bedstead hadn't yet been consumed in the pit-propping process, and then building a small pony truck with flanged wheels to roll along it. This is quite a complex bit of railway engineering, especially as the floor of a hand-dug tunnel is likely to be extremely uneven.

In the modern, uniformly shaped and plastic-lined descendant of Tom, Dick and Harry, it should not be so difficult. The smooth surface means that wheels alone will be able to run freely, so a truck can be made with nothing more than a sheet of board and four castors stolen from the trolley used to take the library books around.

If a trolley speed of 20mph could be achieved, then it will take only twenty-six seconds to travel from the chalet to freedom. However, and allowing for the trolley's return journey, this still means a throughput of one person per minute, taking us back to the seven-day escape cycle outlined above.

However, if a fifteen-truck express could be built using more castors from more discarded trolleys, a throughput of 900 prisoners per hour would be possible with rigorous discipline and an absolute ban on dramatic attacks of claustrophobia from Danny. Under this scenario, Butlins could be emptied in under twelve hours, or between evening porridge and the following day's breakfast.

FRENCH CARAVAN SITE
THE - HOME - RUN
IT'S QUICKER BY TUNNEL

The exact safe top speed for the freedom express will have to be established by careful experiment on the first few runs. There will be one 'danger velocity' at which the natural oscillations of the knackered free-pivoting castors reach a resonant frequency, leading to a massive underground tank-slapper with potentially fatal results.

The home run

On emerging from the French caravan, make your way to Skegness's attractive North Beach, steal a small boat and sail to the neutral Isle of Wight (see chapter six).

Chapter three
how to Fight a Duel

Stop and think before instigating a bar brawl. Perhaps there is a better way.

Before any further discussion of this topic can proceed, a few things need to be made very clear. Duelling is inherently dangerous. Duelling of all forms is also highly illegal, and the brandishing of a genuine sword or functioning black-powder pistol in a public place would be considered a very serious matter. You could very easily end up with one hundred hours' hospital-cleaning community service, which isn't going to make you look like d'Artagnan at all.

Even so, there's a very good case for it. In the modern world, serious disputes can only really be concluded in one of two ways: in brawling, which is unseemly, or in litigation, which is tiresome and expensive. Since both of these things are to be avoided, the modern man finds himself bereft of a suitable social convention by which minor affronts can be redressed, which means that a trifling slight may remain lodged in the heart for a lifetime of bitterness and lingering resentment. It's ridiculous. The whole business could be sorted out before breakfast and then quickly forgotten. Especially if you're dead.

Irish Code Duello

Rule 1 The first offence requires the first apology, though the retort may have been more offensive than the insult. Example: A tells B he is impertinent, etc. B retorts that he lies; yet A must make the first apology, because he gave the first offence, and then (after one fire) B may explain away the retort by subsequent apology.

Rule 2 But if the parties would rather fight on, then, after two shots each (but in no case before), B may explain first and A apologise afterwards. The above rules apply to all cases of offences if retort not of stronger class than the example.

Rule 3 If a doubt exists as to who gave the first offence, the decision rests with the seconds. If they will not decide or cannot agree, the matter must proceed to two shots, or to a hit if the challenger requires it.

Rule 4 When the lie direct is the first offence, the aggressor must either beg pardon in express terms, exchange two shots previous to apology, or three shots followed by explanation, or fire on till a severe hit be received by one party or the other.

Rule 5 As a blow is strictly prohibited under any circumstances amongst gentlemen, no verbal apology can be received for such an insult. The alternatives, therefore, are: The offender handing a cane to the injured party to be used on his own back, at the same time begging pardon; firing until one or both are disabled; or exchanging three shots and then begging pardon without the proffer of the cane. If swords are used, the parties engage until one is well blooded, disabled, or disarmed, or until, after receiving a wound and blood being drawn, the aggressor asks pardon. A disarm is considered the same as a disable. The disarmer may (strictly) break his adversary's sword, but if it be the challenger who is disarmed it is considered ungenerous to do so. In the event the challenged be disarmed and refuses to ask pardon or atone, he must not be killed, as formerly; but the challenger may lay his own sword on the aggressor's shoulder, then break the aggressor's sword, and say, 'I spare your life!' The challenged can never revive that quarrel, – the challenger may.

Rule 6 If A gives B the lie and B retorts by a blow (being the two greatest offences), no reconciliation can take place till after two discharges each or a severe hit, after which B may ask A's pardon for the blow, and then A may explain simply for the lie, because a blow is never allowable, and the offence of the lie, therefore, merges in it. Challenges for undivulged causes may be reconciled on the ground after one shot. An explanation or the slightest hit should be sufficient in such cases, because no personal offence transpired.

Rule 7 But no apology can be received in any case after the parties have actually taken their ground without exchange of fires.

Rule 8 In the above case no challenger is obliged to divulge his cause of challenge (if private) unless required by the challenged so to do before the meeting.

Rule 9 All imputations of cheating at play, races, etc., to be considered equivalent to a blow, but may be reconciled after one shot, on admitting their falsehood and begging pardon publicly.

Rule 10 Any insult to a lady under a gentleman's care or protection is to be considered as, by one degree, a greater offence than if given to the gentleman personally, and to be regulated accordingly.

Rule 11 Offences originating or accruing from the support of ladies' reputations are to be considered as less unjustifiable than any others of the same class, and as admitting of slighter apologies by the aggressor. This is to be determined by the circumstances of the case, but always favourably to the lady.

Rule 12 In simple unpremeditated rencontres with the small-sword, or couteau-de-chasse, the rule is, first draw, first sheathe, unless blood be drawn; then both sheathe and proceed to investigate.

Rule 13 No dumb firing or firing in the air is admissible in any case. The challenger ought not to have challenged without receiving offence, and the challenged ought, if he gave offence, to have made an apology before he came on the ground; therefore children's play must be dishonourable on one side or the other, and is accordingly prohibited.

Rule 14 Seconds to be of equal rank in society with the principals they attend, inasmuch as a second may either choose or chance to become a principal and equality is indispensable.

Rule 15 Challenges are never to be delivered at night, unless the party to be challenged intends leaving the place of offence before morning; for it is desirable to avoid all hot-headed proceedings.

Rule 16 The challenged has the right to choose his own weapon, unless the challenger gives his honour that he is no swordsman; after which, however, he cannot decline any second species of weapon proposed by the challenged.

Rule 17 The challenged chooses his ground, the challenger chooses his distance; the seconds fix the time and terms of firing.

Rule 18 The seconds load in the presence of each other, unless they give their mutual honours that they have charged smooth and single, which should be held sufficient.

Rule 19 Firing may be regulated, first by signal; secondly, by word of command; or thirdly, at pleasure, – as may be agreeable to the parties. In the latter case, the parties may fire at their reasonable leisure, but second presents and rests are strictly prohibited.

Rule 20 In all cases a misfire is equivalent to a shot, and a snap or a non-cock is to be considered a misfire.

Rule 21 Seconds are bound to attempt a reconciliation before the meeting takes place, or after sufficient firing or hits, as specified.

Rule 22 Any wound sufficient to agitate the nerves and necessarily make the hand shake must end the business for that day.

Rule 23 If the cause of meeting be of such a nature that no apology or explanation can or will be received, the challenged takes his ground and calls on the challenger to proceed as he chooses. In such cases firing at pleasure is the usual practice, but may be varied by agreement.

Rule 24 In slight cases the second hands his principal but one pistol; but in gross cases two, holding another case ready charged in reserve.

Rule 25 Where the seconds disagree and resolve to exchange shots themselves, it must be at the same time and at right angles with their principals. If with swords, side by side, with five paces interval.

All matters and doubts not herein mentioned will be explained and cleared up by application to the Committee, who meet alternately at Clonmel and Galway at the quarter sessions for that purpose.

ADDITIONAL GALWAY ARTICLES

Rule 1 No Party can be allowed to bend his knee or cover his side with his left hand; but may present at any level from the hip to the eye.

Rule 2 None can neither advance or retreat if the ground be measured. If no ground be measured, either party may advance at his pleasure, even to the touch of muzzles; but neither can advance on his adversary after the fire, unless the adversary steps forward on him. The seconds on both sides stand responsible for this last rule being strictly observed, bad cases having occurred from neglecting of it.

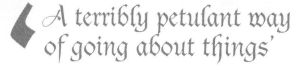

74

The problem is especially galling when it afflicts notables,
celebrities and other public figures. They are inevitably reduced
to sniping at each other in newspaper columns and sensationalist
memoirs, which is a terribly petulant way of going about things. It
is accepted that the pen is mightier than the sword, and that the ink
of the prophet is more sacred than the blood of the martyr,[1] but it
soon becomes rather boring for the rest of us and isn't half as good
to watch. A real man does not bear grudges or indulge in pseudo-
literary sparring. A real man demands satisfaction.

There is another way of looking at this. Since the decline of public
hanging and bear-baiting, there is little to distract the modern citizen
from his or her prescribed daily grind of commuting, labour and
chores. The most that can be expected is some second-rate busking.
So the sight of two people hacking each other to pieces in a public
arena of combat will provide a most pleasing *divertissement*, and
no jury will convict. Samuel Pepys saw fit to record such things in
his diary, as this entry from 17 January 1668 reveals:

> 'Up, and by coach to Whitehall to attend the
> Council there; and here I met... all the discourse
> of the duel yesterday between the Duke of
> Buckingham, Holmes, and one Jenkins on one
> side, and my Lord Shrewsbury, Sir Jo Talbot,
> and one Bernard Howard, on the other side;

1 An old Islamic proverb

and all about my Lady Shrewsbury, who is a
whore and is at this time, and hath for a great
while been, a whore to the Duke of Buckingham
[see Rule 11]; and so her husband challenged
him, and they met yesterday in a close near
Barne Elmes and there fought; and my Lord
Shrewsbury is run through the body from
the right breast through one shoulder, and
Sir J. Talbot all along up one of his arms, and
Jenkins killed upon the place, and the rest all
in a little measure wounded.' [2]

You don't get this sort of thing in *Heat* magazine. Yet.

Duelling – and this is what's good about it – is a formalised
affair and is therefore subject to rules and governed by etiquette.
Regulations for the pursuit of man-to-man combat existed in
antiquity and at the jousting lists of King Arthur's court, but the
first modern treatise emerged from Renaissance Italy in the form of
the *Flos Duellatorum in Armis* ('the flower of battle') in 1410.
Unfortunately it's in Latin, although the pictures are quite good.

The French followed in 1583 with *Le Combat de Mutio
Lustinopolitain*, which, like the Citroën DS and the Common
Agricultural Policy, was far more complex than necessary and

2 Shrewsbury died two months later.

This treatise on unarmed combat pre-dates the invention of trousers.

featured eighty-five rules. It was therefore the simpler, twenty-six-rule Irish Code Duello of 1777 that was adopted by most of Europe and America, and so that is the one reprinted here without permission from the gentlemen of Tipperary, Galway, Sligo, Mayo and Roscommon, who wrote it. [3]

This stuff is worth knowing. During the Czech elections in 2006, Prime Minister Jiří Paroubek sent his arch rival Mirek Topolánek a pair of duelling pistols and a pair of swords, challenging him to a live TV debate. Wrong! If he'd read the Code he would have seen (Rule 16) that it is the challenged man who chooses the weapons, not the challenger. Also, the arrangements were the responsibility of his seconds, not him personally. The man's obviously a poltroon. Apart from anything else, a live TV debate is exactly the sort of thing we're trying to avoid here.

Even so, a certain amount of latitude is necessary if the duel is to be revived in a modern, liberal, egalitarian and multicultural society. Strictly speaking, duelling is a recourse available only to the nobility, since it is a means of defending honour and only an aristocracy elevated to a state of purity by centuries of ripping off the peasants can conceive of having such a thing. If, therefore, you wear coarse boots or went to a comprehensive, you may find yourself being thrashed for your impudence by his lordship's butler. The solution is simple: substitute the twenty-first-century 'respect'

3 Sources for the Irish Code Duello post-date the original by a century or so. It seems likely that there were originally thirty-six rules.

for 'honour', and everyone is fair game. We don't just want to end up with a load of toffs mincing around in the garden.

Similarly, the distinction between gross and slight offences is rather arcane, and can probably be ignored. Other than that, it stands up pretty well. Consider Rule 10. It all sounds a bit Mr Darcy in the frock-coated syntax of 1777, but with a little work it translates convincingly into the vernacular of today, where it emerges as 'Here, are you looking at my bird?' If you were, read on.

Here, then, is a guide to the various stages of organising and campaigning a duel, plus a few useful hints that may help you emerge victorious from the field of honour, smeared with the blood and viscera of your late detractor.

The insult

Technically, this is something over which you have no control. It is simply a matter of waiting until someone accuses you of impertinence (see Rule 1). If you are settling an existing grievance, go straight to The Challenge.

However, if you are a well-liked sort of chap but impatient to stand your ground and display these new skills you may have to take the

'My Lady Shrewsbury, who is a whore'

initiative, though you should remember that Rule 16 stipulates that, as the aggressor, you lose the right to chose the weapons.

Care is needed. The illustration below shows some current British Olympic fencing and shooting athletes, who are to be avoided at all costs. Also, simply walking into a pub and saying 'Oi, tosser' to someone is only likely to instigate a punch-up, unless the other bloke happens to be reading this chapter at the bar. Using the correct language, though, will be a vital clue to any vaguely cognisant victim (and indeed any onlookers) that something more than a smack in the teeth is called for (see Rule 5).

Some prominent shooting and fencing champions – best avoided.

One simple trick is to use the word 'sir' a lot, like they did on *The Bounty*, as this immediately establishes the exchange in the appropriate chronological context; that is, the eighteenth century. So you could try:

> 'Sir. I put it to you, sir, that you are more than adequately versed in the sin of Onan, sir.'

He won't have the square root of a bastard clue what you're on about and will therefore probably call you a twat. This is indeed impertinence, sir, so you're on your way. Well done.

The challenged man is likely to be baffled by the florid script in your speech bubble.

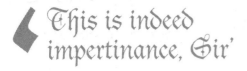
The Challenge

The notion that a duel is instigated by striking your adversary's face with a glove has been greatly misappropriated by the stage and screen, but it does have a historical precedent. When a medieval squire was knighted, he was subjected to a ritual slap in the face with a gauntlet, the implication being that it was the last insult he would have to endure without retaliating. Strictly, you should throw the glove at the feet of your proposed opponent, thereby inviting him to slap *you* with it. This, being a blow, is a gross insult (see Rule 5), especially as, among gentlemen with receding chins and fragile bone structures, the face was strictly off-limits.

Now say 'Sir, I demand satisfaction' and leave immediately in whatever high dudgeon is. From here on it is up to your friends to organise the time and place, and there's an end on 't (Johnson).

The role of the seconds

You must nominate your second with much thought, for, as you will see from Rule 25, he may end up in the fray himself. He must be a valued friend, for he will be charged with preparing your weapon,

but not so valued that you mind losing him, and not anyone who owes you a significant amount of money.

Your second must meet your opponent's second to arrange the time and place of the duel. Customarily, it must be a secluded spot, away from 'constables' and out of sight of the plebs. In British army duels, it was normal to fight in woodland clearings and claim that the meeting was an 'accidental encounter'.

Here, though, we are concerned with providing a spectacle for The People, so suitable locations might include beer gardens, shopping centre concourses and the central reservations of busy dual carriageways.

The weapons

According to American versions of the Irish Code Duello, the default weapon was the sword and the default sword was the rapier. But by the eighteenth century duelling with pistols was more fashionable. These are the two arms we shall consider here.

You will remember (Rule 16) that the challenged man chooses the weapons. This is likely to be the other bloke unless this book proves uncommonly popular. Note, though, that you can decline to fight with blades (Rule 16 again) but will thereby probably end up in a shoot-out, which has the potential to generate a lot more paperwork, admittedly maybe for someone else.

The rapier, which typically has a blade around thirty-six to forty-two inches long, was regarded as a thrusting weapon but could also be sharpened along some or all of its length for cutting strokes. Whichever type you decide on, be sure to buy two the same, as your opponent is unlikely to have one already. If he has, you should be concerned.

Rapiers are relatively easy to come by, and can be found on Internet auction sites. You must be sure you are buying the real thing, and not a floppy stage rapier for use in productions of the *Romeo and Juliet* ballet or, worse, merely a button-ended sport-fencing rapier, which is the roundy-ended scissors of duelling weapons. If shopping online, be absolutely sure that you are not buying a 1967 Sunbeam Rapier.

Duelling pistols are a more expensive proposition. They should be bought as a matched pair and be of the smooth-bored flintlock type. If you decide you don't want a Porsche any more it is possible to buy original, cased and functioning sets of duelling pistols from specialist dealers. But the Internet, again, will provide many modern replica types used by firearms enthusiasts and shooting

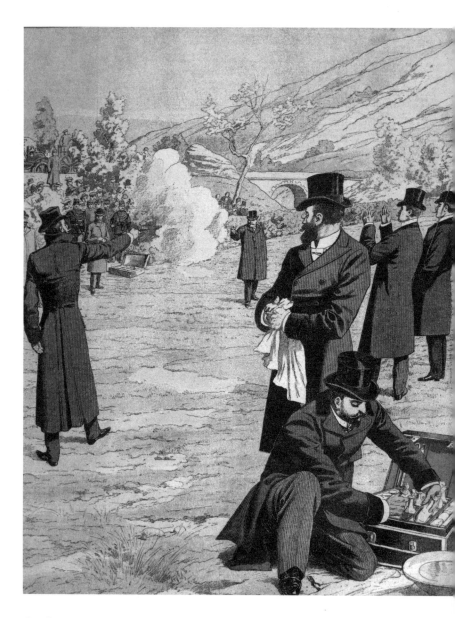

Gentlemen sort it out in a level-headed and reasonable way.

clubs. Be alert to the dangers of buying plastic imitation pistols or non-firing 'decommissioned' examples, and the existence of the American rock band The Duelling Pistols, which has produced a number of CDs.

Marking the ground

Rapier duels are the simplest to organise. The seconds should mark two lines on the ground such that when the two combatants stand on them, the tips of their swords are about two feet apart. The contest is started with a shout of *Allez!* from one of the seconds (or an impartial presiding officer if you're doing this properly). It's then a straightforward matter of hacking away until the crimson fluid is brought forth. If duelling in a built-up area, take theatrical advantage of any tables, display cabinets full of priceless porcelain and chandeliers.

Pistols duels can take more varied and complex forms. Firing may be 'at pleasure' (see Rule 25) or at prearranged signals from the seconds, such as hand claps or the dropping of an exquisitely embroidered silk handkerchief.

Two suggestions from the French rules are worth considering. The first is the duel *au signal*. The protagonists begin up to forty-five

paces apart, and their advance and the discharge of the weapons are regulated by three claps at two-second intervals by a second. At the first clap, they begin advancing, pistols pointing at the floor; at the second, they raise their arms and take aim; at the third, they fire simultaneously.

Better still is the duel *a volonte*. Lines are drawn forty paces apart and again twenty paces apart and centrally between the first two. Starting from the outer lines and on the command *Marche!*, the

Harsh, but fair.

duellists walk towards each other. Either man can stop and take
aim at any time, but may not fire until he reaches the second line.
The first man to reach the second line will have the advantage of
firing first, but if he misses he must then stand his ground until the
other man reaches *his* second line. He will then have the advantage
of firing from closer range. This provides excellent drama and will
have the good-natured bank-holiday crowd on the edge of their
shooting sticks.

HAMMER   FLINT   FRIZZEN   FRIZZEN SPRING

PAN

TRIGGER

POWDER FLASK

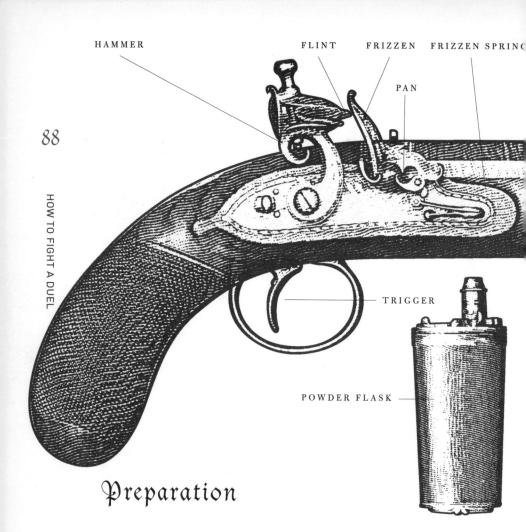

Preparation

If duelling with pistols, then the seconds must charge 'smooth and single' (see Rule 18), meaning that the weapon is smooth-bored and only one ball is in the barrel. Your second should examine your opponent's shooter for evidence of 'French rifling'; that is, spiral grooves cut into the barrel to spin the shot and improve accuracy, but stopping an inch or so short of the muzzle so as to go undetected. This is very bad form.

To load the pistol, first pull the hammer to the 'half cock' position, which allows the pan to be filled but does not allow the gun to be

BARREL

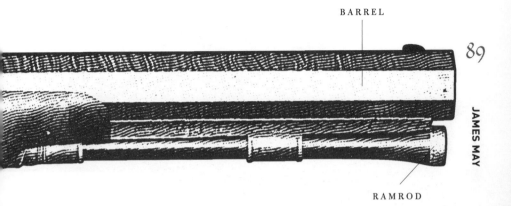

RAMROD

fired. Pour a measure of black powder down the barrel, followed by the ball wrapped in a small piece of cloth or paper. Ram the ball home. It should feel tight.

Now pour a little powder into the pan. When this is ignited, it will fire the main charge via a small hole in the side of the barrel next to the mechanism. So if this step is not done very carefully, you could end up with nothing more than 'a flash in the pan'.

Finally, snap the pan shut, check that the flint is in place and will strike the 'frizzen', and finally pull the hammer back to the fully cocked position. It is now ready to fire, but might not, because these things are a bit temperamental. But this simply adds to the inherent jeopardy that helps make a pistol duel so entertaining for everyone else.

If fighting with rapiers, there is nothing much to do apart from to make sure the other bloke's isn't significantly longer than yours.

The duel!

As you step up to your line, torso bared to demonstrate to your opponent that you are not wearing any unsporting armour, one consideration must be foremost in your mind; ahead, even, of any contemplation of your imminent, untimely and probably quite agonising death. And it is this: on the cusp of mortal combat you may be, but you are providing a spectacle.

Stand firm to fire your pistol, sir. It kicks like a mule, in sooth.

And in the battle for the hearts of the assembled throng, language remains your best weapon, as it was for Cyrano de Bergerac. Words like 'treacherous', 'dog', 'varlet', 'charlatan', and 'quisling' will endear you to an audience hungry for the eloquence of a more genteel age.

In fact, literature and film provide a rich source of well-turned phrases that you should collect and reserve for the field of honour. A few to get you going:

> 'Damn you, sir, it's death' (The Duke of Wellington, *Waterloo*)

> 'Very well, look your last upon the sun' (Sir Walter Scott, *Ivanhoe*)

> 'I will run you through, sir' (*The Bounty*)

> 'Prepare to taste cold steel' (Various Commando picture books. Do not use in pistol duels)

> 'This tongue that runs so roundly in thy head should run thy head from thy unreverent shoulders' (William Shakespeare, *Richard II*)

Any one of these may disarm thine enemy long enough for you to slip in a lethal thrust or shot.

Skewer the scurvy blackguard through the midden'

In a rapier duel, a number of moves are available to the practised swordsman but two are vitally important here. The first is the parry, by which you will deflect the oncoming blade (below) and then there is the lunge, which is effected by straightening the back leg and the 'off hand', doubling up the other leg and extending the weapon arm in a flash to skewer the scurvy blackguard through the midden (below right).

The parry (left) and the lunge (right).

When firing a flintlock pistol, do not be alarmed by the initial burst of fire and smoke from the ignited pan, which may cause you to falter and miss. Compared with a modern breech-loaded handgun, there will be a noticeable delay between the fall of the hammer and the actual discharge of the round and, short though the interval may be, it is long enough to skew your aim. Also, the flintlock action will be relatively stiff, and the pressure of your quaking finger on the trigger may turn the barrel slightly to the right and cause you to fell a spectator.

When you fall, mortally wounded, and even though you sense that you are smitten through the helm and, without help, cannot last till dawn (*Morte d'Arthur*), you must remain steadfast and unbowed. At school, they told you that a thorough reading and analysis of Shakespeare's *Macbeth* would stand you in good stead one day, and the moment has finally arrived. With your last exhalation, say:

> 'He has killed me, mother.'
> [Dies]

𝔓ostscript

In October 2002, prior to the eventual US invasion of Iraq, the Iraqi vice president Taha Yassin Ramadan, acting as second to Saddam Hussein, proposed that the whole issue be settled by a duel between the two countries' presidents, with Kofi Annan acting as presiding officer. George Bush declined the challenge and therefore, according to duelling convention, is a dishonourable coward. So technically, Iraq won.

The man on the right was hanged, but the one on the left was lucky not to be shot.

NONE OF THAT ANTENATAL PARENTING RUBBISH HAD PREPARED ME FOR WHAT WAS ABOUT TO HAPPEN!

As we have seen so far, the modern male is woefully ill-equipped for those defining trials of manhood that can confront him at any moment, but nowhere is he quite so damningly unprepared as he is for the everyday miracle of childbirth.

You may be a father already, and feeling smug about the antenatal classes you attended in the school hall, and how supportive you could be, and how you always knew what's best for baby. But be honest; did you ever really learn what to do if it was you, the man who put that deposit in the sacred vault of humankind's future in the first place, who had to see the job through?

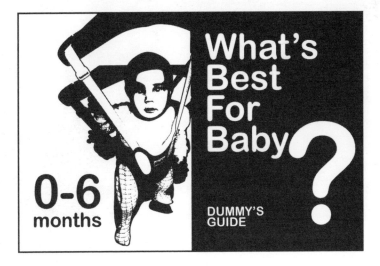

And the rest of us, the childless ones, are pathetically impotent when measured against the demands of obstetrics. At school you may have learned mouth-to-mouth resuscitation, how to put someone in the recovery position, and how to stem the blood flow from a serious wound. But of midwifery? Rarely anything, beyond a dim understanding that it will involve some warm water and towels. It's as if it's no concern of ours. But it could be.

In Britain alone there are around 15 million women of childbearing potential randomly distributed throughout the land, from the inner city to the remote farmstead. With that in mind, the incidence of maternity hospitals and rosy-cheeked district nurses in Morris Minors begins to look woefully sparse.

This country sees around 700,000 births a year, or the best part of 2000 *a day*. Despite what your grandmother calls 'the wonderful things they can do nowadays' there will always be miscalculations. Add to this premature births, cancelled trains, breakdowns, bad weather or simple incomprehension and there's no escaping the terrifying reality that some women are going to be caught short. It happens more often than you might imagine.

Labour can last for days, in which case there's a fair chance you'll be able to find professional help. You should. But it can, especially in second and third births, be over in a matter of hours, and if the storm is raging outside and all hope of rescue is lost, you'll have no choice but to roll your sleeves up and welcome the squawking infants into the world yourself. You need to know this stuff, or you are little better than a vessel for maintaining sperm at its correct operating temperature.

The delivery of twins is a perfect scenario with which to begin your enlightenment. For a start, it places an extra onus on you, because you must remember to record which child is born first, since it has a bearing on the matter of succession. You, effectively, could decree which one inherits the estate and which one ends up in the army. The gestation period for twins is typically three weeks shorter than it is for a single foetus, and twins are more likely to be born prematurely. They are also slightly more likely to be afflicted by breech delivery and umbilical cord problems. Generally, if you are mentally prepared for twins – which account for around one in 70 conceptions[1] – one baby will be a doddle. If it's triplets or more, you will already be an old hand by the time the third one comes along.

But be assured that this manual is not a thinly disguised exhortation to become a new-age post-feminist male who understands the occult mysteries of the menses and all that nonsense. That stuff helps no one save the publishers of wishy-washy condescending 'parenting' magazines. You cannot possibly know what it means to be a woman and should not offend them by trying. Neither do you fully

---

1 About one in 250 conceptions produces identical twins; about one in 5000 will be triplets.

THE BAD NEWS WAS, THERE WERE TWO OF THEM IN THERE!

understand the dark internal labyrinth of plumbing that is the human female's reproductive system, which is a bit like a helicopter. You don't really know how it works, you just know that it does, and any attempt to understand it properly will simply leave you too frightened to go anywhere near it.

Here is what you need to know. The babies have formed in the womb, or uterus, which is at the top of the birth canal, or vagina, just beyond the cervix. Cruelly, God has decreed that they should be born into the world, and you can no more delay their advent than Canute could turn back the tide. So what is required of you now is a little cub-scout preparedness in the face of a relatively straightforward practical task. That is all. So do your best.

If you are not ready then, no matter how sympathetic, supportive or *understanding* you may have been in the past, you will have failed woman in her hour or two of greatest need, when every social and civil convention falls away to leave only the bestial terror of a traumatic bodily function; when you must, by contrast, step aside from the inner ape to become a dispassionate guardian of proper procedure and a bedrock of strength and reassurance. This is no time to be a sap.

Remember: nature took care of childbirth, and humankind flourished, long before science took an interest in the matter. In the era of *Tess of the d'Urbervilles* a peasant girl might squat in the field to deliver her baby and then gather herself up to get on with the harvest. Birth is not an aberration or even, in the minds of most doctors, a medical emergency. It was going on while we were still swinging through the trees and instinct will serve the mother better than anything else. So don't panic.

But it must also be acknowledged that until a few generations ago, and even in the most developed countries, infant and mother mortality was a depressing reality that made the very act of conception something of a gamble. The usual causes were malnutrition and disease, but ignorance of a few basic birthing precautions added to the toll. You must not add to it further through your timorousness, squeamishness or ham-fistedness. Be steadfast, and remind yourself of what the poor woman is going through. She is about to pass a whole human infant through a bodily opening well-served with nerve endings that would normally fit snugly around your thumb. Consider that, and then pull yourself together. The worse that can happen to you is that your shirt will be ruined.

The action begins with the release of a hormone, oxytocin, which informs the mother's body that the nutritional needs of her burden can no longer be met by the placenta that has sustained them for the last nine months. It also kick-starts the contractions and the softening of the tissues in the cervix. The most obvious evidence that all this is going on will be when the waters break, the 'waters' being a membranous sac of amniotic fluid surrounding the babies in the womb. The sac ruptures, and the fluid escapes through the cervix. Sometimes it will escape as a gentle trickle over time, but sometimes as a gushing deluge. In rare cases waters can break some weeks before labour begins, and often they will give you twenty-four or even fourty-eight hours' grace in which you can deliver the mother to a hospital and relieve yourself of any further involvement. But they may well break when a quick labour is already well under way, so in fact the waters serve to confirm only that the woman is unequivocally up the duff. Keep calm and carry on, as they used to say in the army.

Find a clean and well-lit area for the birth, cover it with clean linen or even your own clothes if necessary. Modern thinking says that

BUT SOMETIMES AS A GUSHING DELUGE'

giving birth from a position leaning against a wall or squatting is preferable, because gravity works with you and unhelpful pressure on the birth canal is relieved. But if you are the only other person present, the old-fashioned lying down approach might be safer, otherwise you could fulfil a criticism of a child in later life by allowing it to fall on its head when it was a baby.

Ask the mother to remove all her lower clothing and then cover her, for modesty's sake, with a blanket or similar. If you've never met her before, reassure her that though you are not a doctor, you have read a book, so everything will be fine.

Now bare your arms and wash yourself thoroughly from your fingertips all the way to your elbows with hot water and soap. Infection is the greatest threat in a process that will involve plenty of bleeding. Midwives use alcoholic hand sterilisers for this job, but don't despair. Statistically, you are more likely to be near a bar than a hospital, and neat vodka is an excellent antiseptic. Once you are clean, do not touch anything other than the mother and the baby.

Professionals divide the forthcoming birth into three stages. In the first, the uterus begins to contract in short bursts and moves downwards in the pelvis. At the same time the tissues of the cervix soften, and it begins to dilate to allow the babies through.

107

JAMES MAY

The second stage is the movement of the babies through the birth canal and into the world, and the one during which you can be of most help. Finally, the placenta (or afterbirth), the offal-like bag of nutrients linked to the babies by umbilical cords, will be delivered. Twins will usually have a placenta each, but some pairs of identical twins will be connected to a common one.

THAT 'ALARMING BULGING' CAME AS A SHOCK!

There's not much you can do during the first stage, which could last for many hours, other than to offer words of encouragement. If you are of a sporting disposition and own a chronograph wristwatch, you can time the regularity of the contractions. When the interval between them has reduced to about two minutes, the first of the siblings has decided to make like a baby and head out. The cervix will have dilated to a diameter of about four or five inches. You should be able to see it, along with an alarming bulging around the opening of the vagina.

There will probably be a pause before the contractions of the actual birth begin. When they do, they will be more violent, more painful (for her) and may well occasion some blasphemy. The first baby is moving through the cervix and vagina. With each push it will advance through the pelvic area and then retreat a little, but as long as the net effect is advance, there's nothing to worry about. Eventually, you will (hopefully, but more of that in a minute) see the top of its head. This is known as 'crowning'.

It is now essential to slow down the delivery, to prevent rupture of the perineum. Press your thumb gently in this area and instruct the mother to pant rather than push.

Once the baby's head is out support it with your hand and make sure its nose and mouth are free of mucus that might obstruct them. Wipe the baby's face *gently* – it's not even fully born yet, for Pete's sake – with a clean, damp cloth. There is a chance that, as the head appears, you will find the umbilical cord wrapped around the baby's neck, which is potentially dangerous. If possible, but without tugging, slip it over the head. If this is not possible leave it where it is, but be ready to insert a finger underneath it to pull it away from the neck. Obvious, really.

Next guide the shoulders out, one at a time, holding the baby steady so that it does not burst out and cause damage. Do not hold it back, but do not pull it either. If it seems stuck press firmly at the base of the mother's abdomen and politely request more pushing. As the shoulders emerge the baby will turn naturally on to its side, and once the shoulders are free it will slip out quite quickly. Keep hold of it, and keep it tilted slightly head down but *do not* hold it by its feet. This is only for comic strips.[2]

Even if the baby decides on a buttock-first arrival there is nothing much to worry about. Newborn babies are among the bendiest objects in creation; their joints are not even fully formed. Simply keep a lookout for the umbilical cord and remember the face-wiping duty. It will probably come arse/feet/head first. The head is still the biggest part so don't neglect the perineum-pressing bit mentioned above.

Now it is in the world a subtle shift in the baby's operating mechanism will cause it to start breathing with its lungs instead of absorbing oxygen from the blood supply in the umbilical. Check again that its nose and mouth are free of crud. If you are in any doubt, place your mouth over them and give a slight but sharp suck to dislodge any stubborn stuff. By now this bloodied bundle of supposed joy should be wailing like a banshee, but if not *do not* slap its arse. That's a myth. Lie it face down and tickle its spine and flick the soles of its feet with your fingers. Both of these excite the brain and should start the breathing and blubbing. In extreme cases

---

2 Similarly, never hold a rabbit by its ears alone, unless it's dead.

a little mouth-to-mouth resuscitation can be tried by delivering small puffs of air through the nose and mouth. But not too hard. You are not trying to inflate it, merely to trigger the natural breathing response.

Now you can tie off the umbilical cord a few inches from the baby's navel, using a (cleaned) shoelace or a piece of string. This is not absolutely essential, as long as you keep the baby tilted head down, and some midwives advise against it. What is important is that you don't yank on the cord, as this could dislodge the placenta before it's ready and cause potentially fatal internal bleeding in the mother.

Certainly do not think of *cutting* the cord yet. You don't know if there will be one placenta or two, or if one of them or another baby is coming next. So if possible, lie the first baby on the mother's abdomen and keep them warm. Remember to tell her what sex it is. You should be able to work this out by now.

If it's another baby, you already know what to do. If it's a placenta, simply relax and let it come. It's soft and squidgy and a relatively easy job for the mother. It must never be pulled out. Once you have a full complement of babies and placenta, encourage the mother

I RECORDED THAT JACK CAME FIRST. HE OWES ME!

to breast-feed. It stimulates uterine recovery and – here we go – *it's best for baby.*

If the ambulance or a hospital is less than an hour away, leave the placenta attached. The midwife will want to examine it anyway. But if you really are stuck in the sticks you may have to cut the cords. Tie them, as instructed above, a few inches from each baby's navel. Then tie them again, a few inches further out

'A SLIGHT BUT SHARP SUCK TO DISLODGE ANY STUBBORN STUFF'

than that. Cut in between the ties with scissors or knife, which you should sterilise with your vodka or a flame.[3] The umbilical is quite tough and gristly but the mother cannot feel it, so be firm.

And that's it, save perhaps for a little abdominal massage to speed the recovery of the ravaged uterus. Congratulations. A man may take a life, a man may even save one, but his condition admits of no privilege greater than to ensure that a new one starts healthily. Now go to the pub. It's traditional.

And don't ever moan again about having to wrap up some Christmas presents.

AS YOU MUST HAVE SAID YOURSELF SISTER – PUSH!

3 The blue flame of a gas oven is 'cleaner' than the yellow one of a cigarette lighter or match. Use that if you can.

CHAPTER FIVE

Driver Bob Deeth sounded his whistle, pulled gently on the handle of his regulator, and eased the massive Merchant Navy steam locomotive 35008 *Orient Line* out of London's Waterloo station en route to Southampton, hauling the day's boat train.

To our twenty-first-century imagination, fuddled by misty-eyed nostalgia for the glory of the steam era, this is an image of sunny and gleaming loveliness; of supreme dignity made machine, proud and polished. But it didn't seem that way at the time.

The year was 1967, the month July, and the final demise of mainline British steam traction was but a year away. The once-cheered Merchant Navy had become a ruin of an engine, filthy, clapped out, unloved, minimally maintained and operating under the shadow cast by the scrapman's cutting torch, which had already despatched much of Britain's twenty-thousand-strong steam locomotive fleet.

The Merchant Navy clanked defiantly southwards. Clear of London's conurbation and its speed limits, the crew coaxed it onwards, stoking its ravaged boiler mercilessly. Doubtless it leaked a bit, the bearings of wheels and motion work were terminally worn out, and *Orient Line* had been kept in service only by cannibalising those of its sisters already in the scrapyard. Yet somehow, somewhere along the journey,

The end of steam was ignominious. Its second coming will be shrouded in clouds of glory.

this neglected heap of anachronistic ironmongery hit 102mph. This
was such a bold, audacious and frankly foolhardy driving exploit that it
is still recounted in reverential tones whenever old railwaymen meet.

Driver Deeth was twenty-eight years old.

A few decades earlier, the idea of such a lad driving a Top Link express
locomotive would have been unthinkable. Their drivers were usually
fifty-year-old veterans occupying a position of great prestige and
commanding hard-earned respect. This is why, in A.P. Thompson's
famous 1932 poster advertising the *Flying Scotsman* service from
London, the driver is placed high up in a stylised engine given the
proportions of a church, and the awestruck onlooker on the platform
is diminished to a few feet in height.

But by 1967 the veterans were firmly ensconced in the comfortable
cabs of diesel-electric engines such as the Deltic and Class 47,
relieved to be free, finally, of the squalor of the steam footplate.
Deeth's fledgling presence on the Merchant Navy was a testament to
the low estimation in which steam locomotives had come to be held.

In brutally analytical terms, steam in Britain outstayed its welcome by
at least a decade. The first Clean Air Act of 1956 had identified steam
traction as one of the sources of the choking pea-souper that had
killed 8000 of London's inhabitants in the 'Great Smog' of 1952. It is

The driver of a steam locomotive looks down upon a mere mortal, as indeed he should.

LNER

TAKE ME
BY
THE
FLYING
SCOTSMAN

LEAVES
KING'S CROSS
AT 10 A.M.
EVERY WEEK-DAY

WITH APOLOGIES
TO THE
SOUTHERN RAILWAY

said that you cannot stand anywhere in the British Isles and be more than a hundred miles from the sea; there was a time when you could not stand anywhere in the British Isles and be out of earshot of the whistle of a steam train, and with the whistle came the muck. Coal firing of steam engines, the domestic hearth and suburban power stations were why buildings we now know in their cleaned-up form, such as the Albert Hall and Westminster Abbey, used to be black.

The post-war desire for modernity increasingly embraced clean, efficient and convenient internal combustion, not just on the railways but in the ominous and ever more accessible family car. Steam seemed like a Victorian hangover.

Even a decade before Deeth's exploit, steam power did not sit well with the image of high glamour rail travel could sometimes muster. Passengers in the Pullman coaches of the Atlantic Coast Express in the 1950s enjoyed sumptuous upholstery, exquisite marquetry panels, tasselled curtains, individual ornate table lamps and fine dining from

The last word in luxury and the first word in squalor – both available on the same train.

crisp linen, served by sharply pressed staff. In such surroundings, it would have been difficult to comprehend the medieval toil being endured by the crew hauling them; the constant fug of coal dust blown up from the tender, the heat, the all-pervading grease, the brutal bucking of the crudely sprung locomotive and, when an incline beckoned, the inferno's demand for offerings of coal as fast as a stout man could wield a shovel. In an era when showers were virtually unknown to working men, and even baths were rare, the grime of locomotive operation would have stayed in the pores for a working lifetime, and cleanliness was a goal of retirement.

Steam locomotives were dirty, woefully inefficient, temperamental, expensive to run, time-consuming to prepare for work and satanic in their demands on men. When the end finally came, few people who had worked them for a living mourned their passing.

And yet…time has cleaned the image of steam for us, as surely as it cleaned the smut-caked facades of famous stations. Viewed through the filter of sentiment, and helped by the Brasso and fresh paint of conservationists, the steam locomotive seems like a lost expression of grandeur and everyday pomp, its driver and firemen like gleeful boys given a giant train set to play with. The steam locomotive lingers in the popular imagination like no other obsolete machine.

It helps that the classic steam engineman's pose – elbow jutting from the cab, soot-streaked face peering out and vignetted by a cloud of spent steam, one hand on the whistle – is the most manful that man ever struck. Dr Johnson told us that 'Every man thinks meanly of himself for not having been a soldier', but steam locomotives hadn't been invented then. Today, many of us feel faintly inadequate when measured against a chap whose gnarly hands have ministered to metal dragons. Now, though, this failing can be redressed.

The call of the footplate is louder today than it has been for two generations of railway working. The 'heritage railway' movement has gained more momentum than a runaway train, and the number of restored steam locomotives continues to grow. Steam is now once again seen regularly on the main line, and simple extrapolation suggests that, eventually, those organisations that stoke our innate fascination with the age of steam will eventually join up and serve the whole country. And why not? Historic railways are the best-run railways in Britain, not least because they are the work of people who actually like trains.

The greatest irony is this. One of the newest locomotives running on British metals is No. 60163 *Tornado*, an A1 Pacific of 1947 design but built from scratch by enthusiasts over a nineteen-year period and first steamed in 2008. This may be the future. We may need more drivers for steam trains.

Add to that renewed interest in holidaying in Britain, and the wise man will realise that he must be ready when the regulator beckons and thirteen carriages full of excitable families are trusting his steady hand to haul them safely and happily to the seaside.

Should you find yourself in this position, here is what you need to know.

A locomotive crew with an air of supreme dignity that the rest of us should aim for.

STEAM LOCOMOTIVE BASICS

Steam technology, despite the two-hundred-plus years of refinement manifested in a modern engine like *Tornado*, is essentially an eighteenth-century affair[1] and therefore readily understood. In reality the steam engine is powered by coal, which is used to heat water inside a sealed boiler to create steam at high pressure.

The boiler is a bit more than just a hollow barrel with a fire under one end. Boiler tubes, as pioneered by Stephenson on his *Rocket*, transfer the hot gases from the firebox through the boiler to the chimney, thereby dramatically increasing the surface area exposed to the water. This is why the firebox is at one end and the chimney at the other.

You might wonder why the crew work at the back of the engine, when the view would be much better from the front. Technically, they could work from the front, but where would you put the supplies of fresh coal and water? They have to go in the tender, which would now have to be pushed in front rather than towed behind, exposing the crew to even more coal dust at speed and making visibility even worse. And it's already pretty poor.[2]

The steam collects at the highest point of the boiler, the steam dome, and from there is directed via the regulator to the cylinders, where it acts on pistons and pushes them back and forth inside their cylinders.

1. Please do not write in to remind me of the work of Hero, Savery et al, or later developments in the steam turbine field by Parsons. I know. I'm talking about reciprocating piston steam engines as pioneered by James Watt.
2. Small tank engines, which carry their coal in an integral bunker and their water in tanks around the boiler, can run happily in both directions.

Pedants will want me to point out that it's slightly more involved than that, because the steam from the dome also passes through a superheater, a further arrangement of hot tubes that dries out the wet or 'saturated' steam and increases its temperature and hence pressure, with obvious benefits to performance.

The pistons' reciprocating motion is converted, via rods and cranks, to rotary motion at the wheels. At the same time, other cranks and offsets operate more rods to work the valves controlling the flow of fresh steam to, and exhaust steam from, the cylinders, and in a way that is geometrically baffling to anyone not descended directly from Euclid.

The exhaust steam from the cylinders is directed up the chimney through something known as the 'blast pipe'. This creates a partial vacuum in the boiler tubes and draws a draught through the firebox. This invigorates the hot coals and, almost as importantly, prevents the fire from blowing back into the cab and incinerating the fireman. More of this later.

Tornado's three cylinders are 'double acting', meaning that, unlike in a car engine, the pistons are driven in both directions. When the engine pulls away from rest you will therefore hear six distinct exhaust chuffs for every revolution of the driving wheels. During high-speed running they will blur almost seamlessly into one glorious and continuous chuff that goes on for miles and bloody miles, eeh, and it's right grand 'n' all.[3]

3. In my mind all steam enthusiasts are from Lancashire. Probably because of Fred Dibnah.

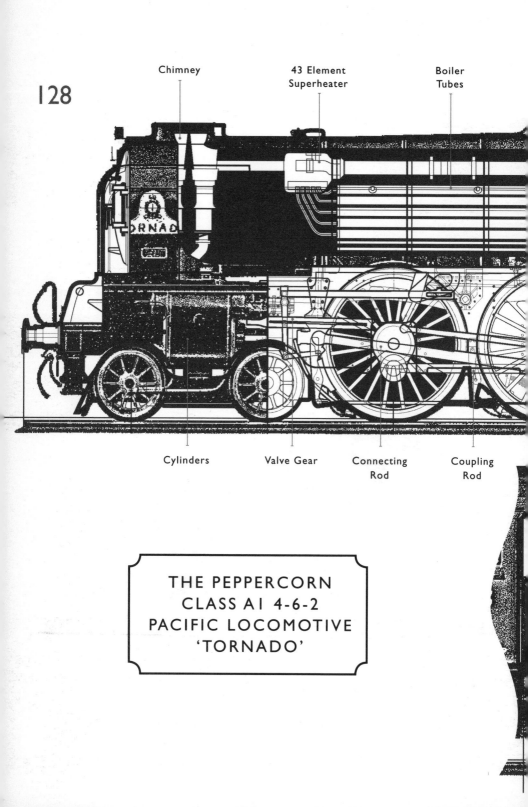

Chimney

43 Element Superheater

Boiler Tubes

Cylinders

Valve Gear

Connecting Rod

Coupling Rod

THE PEPPERCORN
CLASS A1 4-6-2
PACIFIC LOCOMOTIVE
'TORNADO'

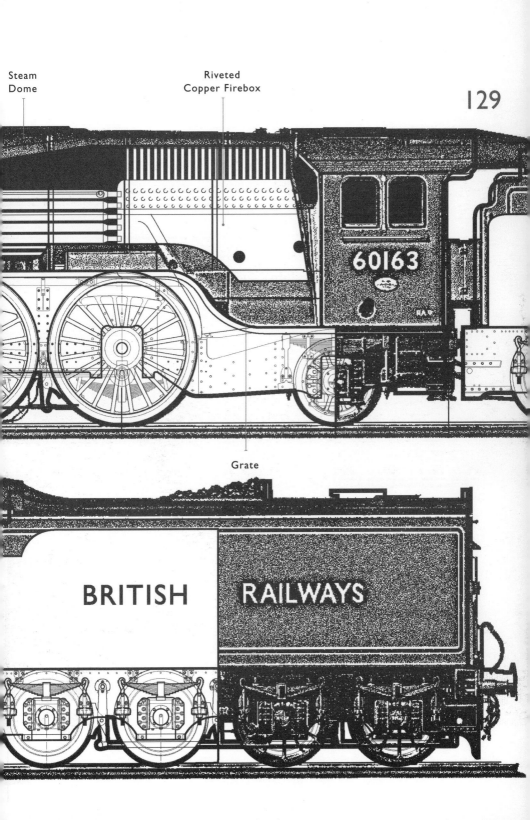

Steam
Dome

Riveted
Copper Firebox

60163

Grate

BRITISH RAILWAYS

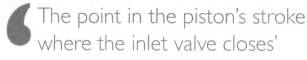
It might seem surprising that the stuff coming from the spout of your kettle can take 600 tons of train from rest to 100mph, but that's because it's not the same stuff. What you can see coming from the kettle, and being exhausted through the locomotive's chimney, is actually water vapour, which is partly condensed steam. Superheated steam exists at around 350°C, is completely invisible, and would probably shatter your teapot.[4]

THE CONTROLS

There are three basic controls used in driving the locomotive, although you shouldn't let that fool you into thinking it's in any way simple. They are:

THE REGULATOR: this controls the amount of steam being fed to the cylinders. It's a sort of throttle. The further you pull it out, the more steam you get.

THE SCREW REVERSER: this is a bit more esoteric. Rotating this alters the geometric relationship between the movement of the pistons and the movement of the valves, affecting something called 'steam cut-off'. 'Cut-off' is the point in the piston's stroke where the inlet valve closes: 'late' cut-off provides more grunt and is used for pulling away and climbing gradients, but as steam continues to expand after the valve is closed, is wasteful of energy. 'Early' cut-off introduces

4. If you look carefully at the spout of a vigorously boiling kettle you may see, or rather not see, true steam in the form of a small gap between the spout and the start of the vapour cloud. Only if you've got absolutely nothing else to do.

just a whiff of steam at the beginning of a piston's stroke and is used when running, when only a small amount of power is needed to keep the train going. Positions in between the two extremes will be used for acceleration and climbing gradients.

Think in terms of pushing a broken-down car. You have to push very hard to get it rolling – late cut-off – but once it's going you can relax a bit – early cut-off.

The reverser's setting is indicated on the gleaming brass sector plate. It works in both directions and cut-off is expressed as a percentage from 0 to 75. With the pointer in the middle the valves are at 'mid-gear' and the engine will not run in either direction. Intelligent use of the reverser is the key to efficient running and saving the labours of your long-suffering but uncomplaining fireman.

THE TRAIN BRAKE: on *Tornado*, this is a departure from original 1940s A1 practice, being a modern air brake. It applies all the wheel brakes on the train and is a proportional control, so the further you turn the handle, the harder the brakes are applied. It is marked in stages: 'initial', 'full service' and 'emergency'. Pretty obvious, really.

Those are the basic going and stopping controls. You will also need to understand the following otherwise, despite *Tornado*'s apparent invincibility, you will quickly break it, and then the people who spent

INSIDE THE CAB

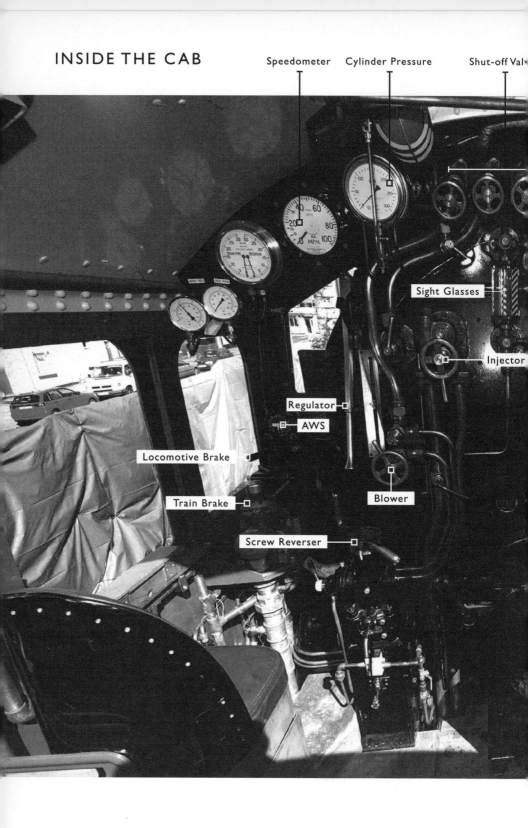

Speedometer

Cylinder Pressure

Shut-off Valve

Sight Glasses

Injector

Regulator

AWS

Locomotive Brake

Train Brake

Blower

Screw Reverser

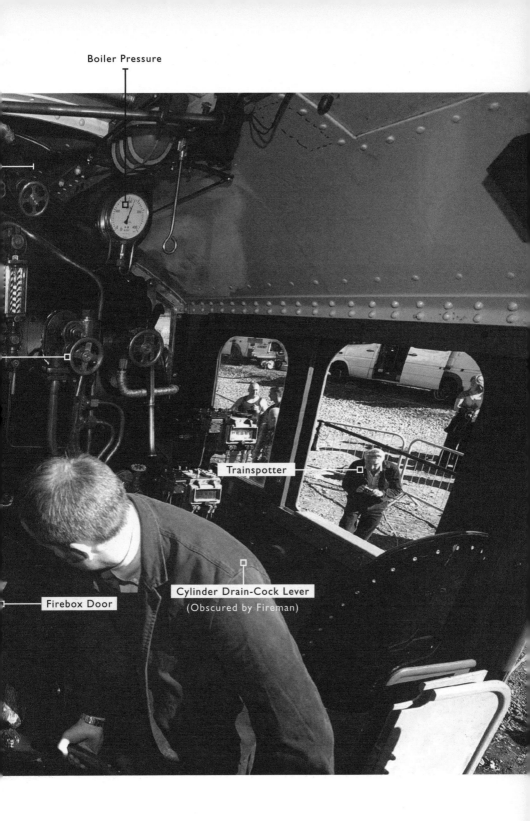

Boiler Pressure

Trainspotter

Cylinder Drain-Cock Lever
(Obscured by Fireman)

Firebox Door

almost two decades building it will fire the boiler with your battered corpse and lubricate their cross-head slides with your molten fat.

SIGHT GLASSES: indicate the level of water in the boiler. The taps underneath empty and replenish them as a precaution against blockages and false readings. Because the water sloshes around in the boiler under acceleration or braking, these require interpretation rather than mere reading. In any case, allowing the boiler to run dry will cause it to either buckle or explode, so watch them carefully and if they look in any way low slake the beast's prodigious thirst with…

THE INJECTORS: these are complex steam pumps that force fresh water from the tender into the boiler. The one on the left is driven by 'live' steam, while the more economical one on the right is driven by exhaust steam, but only when the locomotive is under power. Turn anti-clockwise to open. They will only work if…

THE TENDER WATER VALVES: …are open.

THE LOCOMOTIVE BRAKE: an on–off parking brake only, and not to be used for stopping the train.

THE CYLINDER DRAIN COCK LEVER: opens valves on the cylinders to release condensed water that may have collected while stationary. Open after coming to a halt, and close after pulling away.

Water is not compressible, so failure to do this could see the cylinder heads being blown off, along with those of anyone standing nearby.

THE BLOWER: a manual system to supplement the blast-pipe arrangement mentioned earlier. It creates an artificial draught through the firebox to help prevent the fire's gases entering the cab. Should always be on to some extent when under steam, and especially when stationary, as the blast pipe doesn't work without exhaust steam.

SANDERS: used to help pull away on slippery rails. Moving the lever delivers a stream of sand through pipes under the locomotive to the tops of the rails, increasing grip. There are forward and reverse sanders. Avoid using on the move, or sand may work its way into bearings and grind them to a new shape, after which *Tornado*'s owners may do something similar to your face.

AUTOMATIC WARNING SYSTEM (AWS): an audible/visible indicator of signals passed, triggered by magnetic plates in the track. Will automatically bring the train to a halt if ignored. More of this later.

TENDER WATER SPRAY: directs a spray of water over the coal, in a vain attempt to prevent dust.

SLACKING PIPE: a sort of jetwash, giving a spray of steam and water for rinsing out the cab. Do not use on face, as it's quite hot.

MYSTERIOUS VALVES AND TAPS AT THE TOP: used to shut off various gauges for maintenance. Don't worry about them.

PREPARING THE LOCOMOTIVE

For a run from London King's Cross to York with thirteen coaches you will need:

- **7.5 tons of coal, in the tender.**
- **6200 gallons of water, also in the tender, plus another 1500 gallons in the boiler. Even then a watering stop will be required, and unfortunately it works out at Grantham.**
- **A large can of lubricating oil.**
- **A fellow of good character and build to act as your fireman.**

Before starting to build the fire, first ensure that the locomotive is properly parked: locomotive and tender brakes applied, reverser in the mid-gear position, regulator shut, cylinder drain cocks open. Historically, steam engines have been known to set off by themselves during the steaming-up process, and as *Tornado* weighs 165 tons with a full tender you will not be able to stop it by applying your shoulder to a buffer. So as an added precaution hang the 'not to be moved' sign on the side of the cab. That'll stop it.

Your fireman can now start building the fire, but first will have to remove the remains of the previous one. First he must open the hopper under the ashpan, using the lever on the outside. He can also open the damper door, using the lever on the inside. He can manipulate the 'rocking grate' to dislodge clinker and can even shovel the bigger bits back out and throw them through the cab door. But eventually he will have to crawl under the engine and chip away the stubborn stuff using a fire iron. He will emerge looking like some sort of Neanderthal bog dweller.

From cold, the fire is built like a scout bonfire. Start with diesel-soaked rags, cardboard and bits of wood, and gradually add coal until you have an even, brightly glowing covering over the grate. This is around a quarter of a ton. Keep going.

While all this is going on you, as driver, can see to lubrication. All the small oilers must be filled, and oil dribbled into the holes at the bearings indicated on the image (see page 132-3). Also wipe a layer of oil onto the crosshead slides, and yet more onto the connecting and coupling rods to protect them from rust. Wipe oil all over your face. You're going to end up looking like that anyway, and it has excellent moisturising properties.

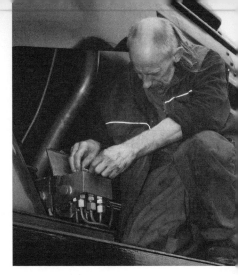

Now an inspector must be
summoned to make a Fitness To
Run report. He will crawl around
and underneath, shining a torch into corners and hitting things. He
is looking for leaks, cracks, and loose bits. He may find the fireman.
Assuming he gives the engine a clean ticket, then it is a simple matter
of waiting for the boiler to reach its working pressure of 250 pounds
per square inch (psi). If starting from cold and being kind to the
engine, this could take a day.

DRIVING

Everything you have read so far is mere theory. A steam locomotive
cannot be driven entirely by the book. They have always been hand-
built in series rather than strictly mass-produced, so not only is every
type different, but every example of every type is different, and will
behave differently on different days. Steam locomotives have foibles
and attitude, like teenagers. They must be felt and understood at a
visceral level. In any case, steam locomotives are driven by two men,
the driver and the fireman, and a unique and apparently psychic
avenue of communication must exist between them.

Engine driving is almost a folk tradition. It is learned by example, and
knowledge is spread by lore in engine sheds and lineside bothies. It

Check the oil level on all automatic lubricators.

is an occult art that comes up through the boots of blokes, and you cannot hope to know it immediately. That said, you may be able to make a fair stab at it if you concentrate.

The most important thing to understand is this: if you drive a car, you will be used to making almost instant responses to the requirement to accelerate, brake, or change down to climb a hill; however, on a steam train, everything takes an age. It takes time for the steam to reach the cylinders when you open the regulator, and it keeps working for a while after you close it. It takes time for the brakes of thirteen coupled coaches to clamp on, and they take their time about coming off again. Speed takes an age to build; stopping distances at any decent speed are measured in multiples of a quarter of a mile.

Steam cannot be made instantly. If coasting downhill under a speed limit but approaching a climb, the fireman might need to shovel madly even though the regulator is closed, in anticipation of demand. A huge amount of forward planning is required, and this is why a special bond must exist between the two men on the footplate. There's no point trying to do this with someone argumentative.

Check that the boiler pressure gauge reads somewhere near 250psi, that the brakes are on, the reverser is in mid-gear and the cylinder drain cocks open. Pull the regulator gently and blow the cylinders through for a few seconds.

If you are starting from a mainline siding or station you will be at a starter signal. When it turns green, wind the reverser to full forward cut-off, release the brakes (don't forget the tender), open the blower, sound the whistle and give the regulator a small tug.

You are looking for a reading of between 50 and 60 on the cylinder pressure gauge. Now shut the regulator again (the steam will continue to expand as the pistons start to move). The locomotive will creak as the drawbar between the footplate and tender is stretched. You will move forward minutely, as yet unaccompanied by any new steam-engine sound beyond the ones *Tornado* was making while it was simmering at rest. Give the regulator another short burst to keep that cylinder pressure constant. Be patient, or the wheels might spin. The train is moving, just.

At some point any second now you will arrive at a spiritual high-point in your life. You will be rewarded with something so deeply moving that it will froth your blood and make your lungs feel bigger; something the memory of which will return to cheer you in old age and melancholy.

Your first chuff. Congratulations. You have just popped your steam-locomotive-driving cherry.

Fortifying chuffs will now come regularly and rhythmically like a jackpot from some weird one-armed bandit of the soul. You can leave the regulator cracked open, but shut the cylinder drain cocks. You may be moving at something like 1mph, and the world will be shrouded in vast billowing clouds of exhaust steam. This looks great, and has the added advantage of obscuring from view all the disturbing-looking railway enthusiasts who have turned out to watch your departure.

Soon you may be doing 5mph, and suddenly your earlier euphoria will be displaced by the terrifying sensation that nearly 700 tons of main line express train is running away with you. Remain calm, sound the whistle again.

Meanwhile, your fireman will be ready to feed the open door to Hades. Firing the engine is not a simple matter of shovelling in coal like a navvy. The grate must be totally covered, which means balletic spadework to throw the coal to left and right, to the back or just behind the firebox door. A good fireman will move more like a fencer than a mere stoker.

He will understand the difference between primary air (drawn *through* the fire from under the grate by opening the damper door) and secondary air (drawn *over* the fire through the firebox door), their effect on burning and steam production, the character of coal, and other things that make him a high priest at the altar of combustion. Firemen seem to say little, but know everything.

The fireman should always watch the sight glasses and be ready to top up the boiler. He should also consider the boiler pressure gauge. For starting off, full pressure of 250psi is needed, but if approaching a stopping station it isn't. There's no point in building Dante's *Inferno* just before coming to a lengthy halt, because the pressure will climb too high and the steam will blow off through the safety valves, which means all his effort has manifested itself as an annoying noise and a light poaching of any trainspotters on nearby bridges.

If the fireman is good, the coal will burn completely and will last longer. A glance at the chimney when cruising is a good indicator of

his performance. If the smoke is black and oily, the engine is effectively running rich and energy in the coal is being wasted. A leaned out and efficient engine produces ethereal, wispy grey smoke.

Tornado is now gathering yet more speed. Keep opening the regulator, and start to wind the reverser back to earlier cut-off. Refer to the cylinder pressure gauge and aim for a constant reading. With 25mph on the speedo something like 45 per cent cut-off should be roughly right, but really this is a matter of feel. Amazingly, your bones will detect the faintest hint of acceleration or retardation, even if it's a gain or loss of just a mile an hour in a minute. This is your best guide.

You might like to think about what to do if you need to stop. Fortunately, modern railway signalling is a bit like road traffic lights, in that there are three colours to worry about: red, yellow and green.

Tornado – made by men from the dust of the earth.

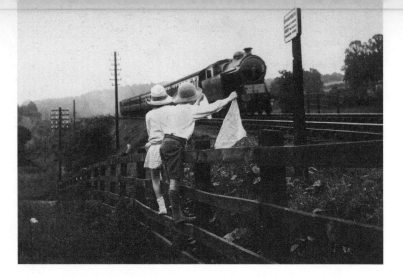

Most modern signals are 'four aspect', meaning there are two yellow lights between the red and the green. The other difference is that because a train at speed could take up to three-quarters of a mile to bring to a complete stop, the light sequence is spread out along the line.

Railways work to something called the 'block section' system. In simple terms, the line is divided into sections, and a train may only enter a section if the previous train has left it.

A green light means that the next three sections at least are clear. The AWS will sound a cheery bell and its circular display will remain black. More regulator! More coal! As the limit of 75mph beckons you can wind the cut-off back to 15–20 per cent. Sound the whistle for sheer joy, wave at children sitting on lineside fences, sing the theme tune from Casey Jones if over forty years old.

Increase cut-off to maintain speed on climbs, close the regulator and open the blower a bit more when running downhill. 'Hills' in railway terms are the faintest of inclines – 1 in 125 is the gradient of the notorious climb over Shap on the Lancaster and Carlisle Railway, and is considered a mountain – but again, you will feel them in your marrow.

The diesel electric locomotive improved many things, but ruined childhood.

A tunnel! Warn the fireman to close the firebox door. Entering
the tunnel at speed can cause a high-pressure blow-back through
the chimney, which could fill the cab with blazing meteors of coal.
Feel the steady thrum of your mount reverberating around ancient
brickwork still stained with the soot of other locomotives long passed
away. Feel the coal dust from the tender swirling around your face
and grinding your eyeballs. Work the tender water spray.

Two yellows means only the next two sections are clear, and there
may be a red after that. Now the AWS sounds a hideous klaxon
and its display turns to the black and yellow 'daisy' pattern, and
you must acknowledge it within 2.7 seconds by pressing the silver
lever on the right of the box. If you fail to do this, the system will
assume you have died or fallen out, and emergency braking will be
applied automatically. Then your passengers will be showered with
champagne and small pieces of meticulously prepared *amuse bouche*
from large and otherwise empty plates, and will want a refund.

Close the regulator, open the blower, coast down to 40mph, applying
gentle train braking if required. If you see a single yellow next, then only
one section is definitely clear. Reduce to 25mph, and be ready for the red.

The AWS: solid means carry on, daisy means be ready to stop.

If it's green, full steam ahead: increase cut-off, open the regulator, exhort your fireman to sate the craving in the raging belly of the monster.

Eventually, you will have to stop completely at Grantham. Do this progressively, remembering that as the train slows the braking requirement diminishes. Work the handle subtly, aiming to reduce braking to nothing as the whole thing comes to an absolute stop. Now put all the brakes on, set the reverser to mid-gear, and cook bacon on a shovel heated in the firebox while the tender is refilled.

A shovel has never been used to such heroic effect.

JAMES MAY

You know how to pull away now. Smile from the cab window in a relaxed and confident way. Not much happens in Grantham, so the platforms will be full of railway buffs with cameras. Once, their work might have turned up decades later as a grainy snapshot in *World of Steam* magazine. Today, it will be on YouTube within hours, complete with any unwarranted blasphemy.

Onwards, then, to York, a hub of our great railway heritage, and home to the world's greatest railway museum, from which other great engines sometimes steam forth – Stephenson's *Rocket*, *Flying Scotsman*, *Oliver Cromwell*, *City of Truro*; legends all, marking their passage into the present with beautiful white plumes in the sky, just as you are doing.

With your hand on the regulator you are a conduit for the wisdom of a dynasty of engine drivers stretching back to Richard Trevethick. Listen to them. Listen to your living locomotive. It will seem happy when you have the settings right and will pant like a well-exercised dog. Get it wrong and it will huff and puff like a stroppy platform luggage porter.

And as you pull up in York, to cheers and adulation, take a moment to reflect on the change that has come over you. You have crossed a line dividing your life into two distinct parts: that time when you had never driven a steam locomotive, and this new age of man, when you have.

Chapter Six

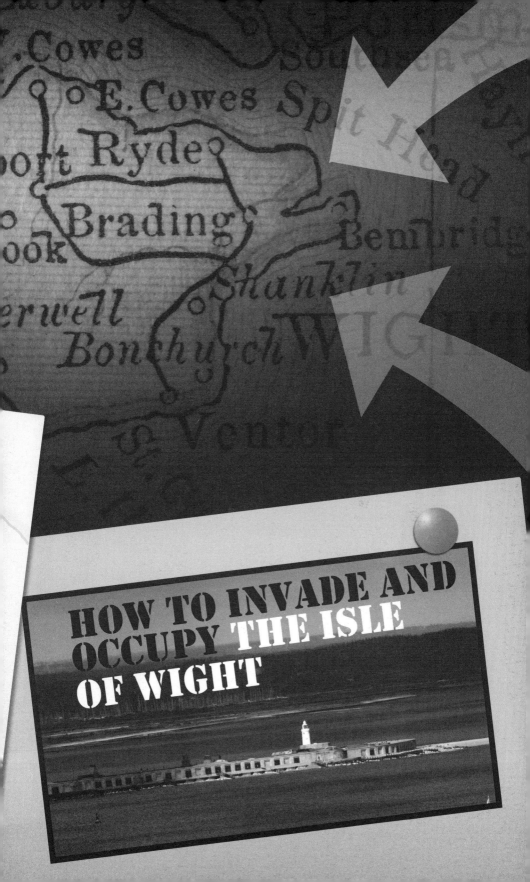

HOW TO INVADE AND OCCUPY THE ISLE OF WIGHT

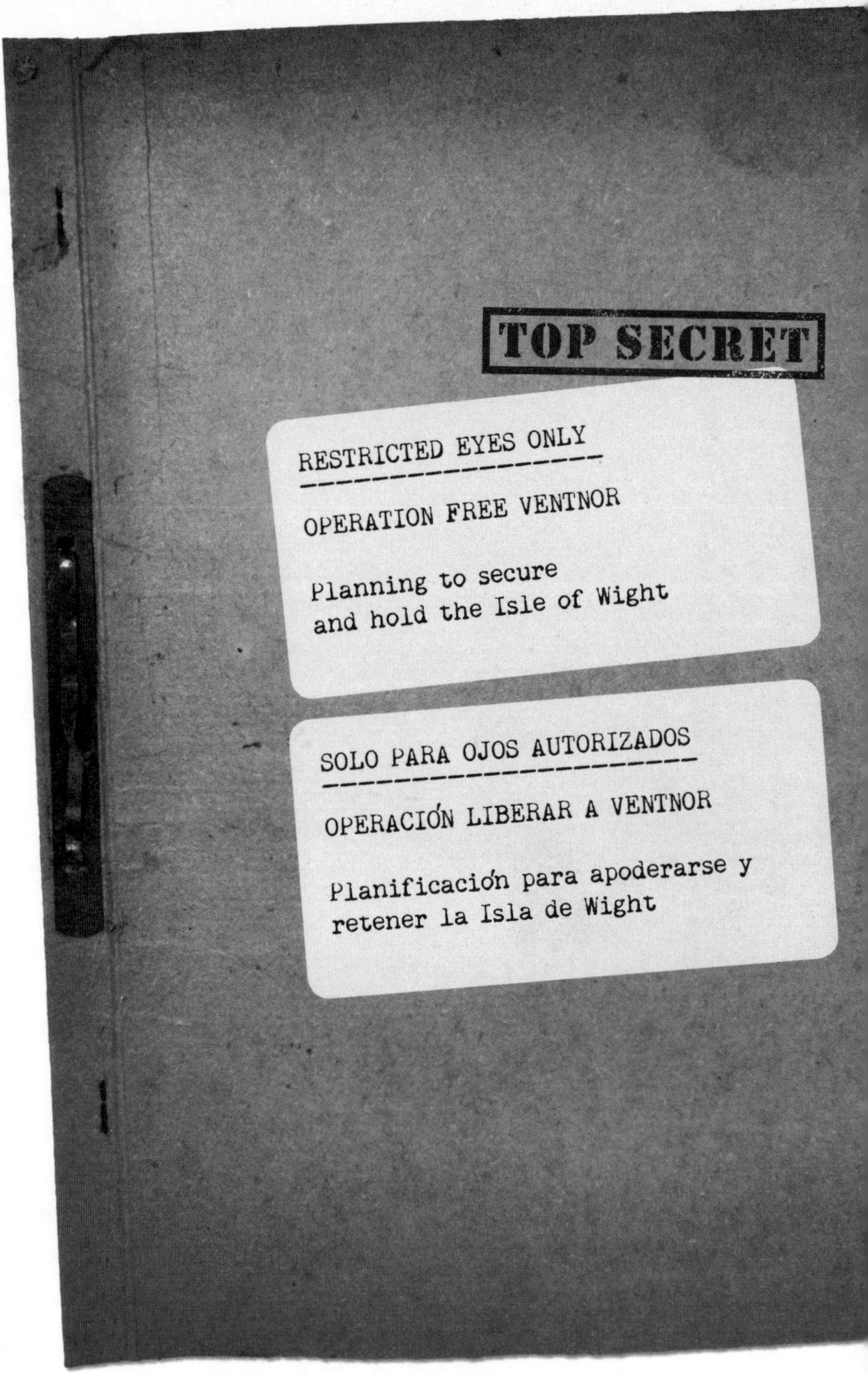

TOP SECRET

RESTRICTED EYES ONLY
—————————————————

OPERATION FREE VENTNOR

Planning to secure
and hold the Isle of Wight

SOLO PARA OJOS AUTORIZADOS
——————————————————————————

OPERACIÓN LIBERAR A VENTNOR

Planificación para apoderarse y
retener la Isla de Wight

It isn't widely known,[1] but in 1981 a detailed strategy was drawn up for an Argentine invasion of the Isle of Wight. This in itself sounds quite disturbing, but more so when you learn that the plan was conceived by the British government.

With diplomatic relations regarding the sovereignty of the Malvinas becoming extremely strained, Margaret Thatcher's cabinet gave serious consideration to allowing General Galtieri to storm Wight instead. Following a token and carefully choreographed phoney counter-attack by British forces campaigned purely for the sake of appearances, the Argentineans would be allowed a free hand on the island in return for leaving the Falklands alone.

Everyone, it was reasoned, would be happy. Argentina would enjoy the kudos of triumphing over the hated British, Britain would be spared the inconvenience and massive expense of sending a task force thousands of miles to liberate a useless lump of rock covered in penguins, and the people of the Isle of Wight probably wouldn't notice.

1. And isn't actually true. I'm obliged by the lawyers to put this bit in.

An early draft of the scheme recently came to light at the back of a cupboard in the members' bar of a golf club near Chequers, along with some unpaid tabs. Parts of it are reproduced here without permission and at great risk.

At first, this rough, typewritten treatise was dismissed as the work of a deluded quasi-military fantasist or, at best, an elaborate student hoax. But further investigation has suggested that it was typewritten simply because the only computers available in 1981 were the BBC and Commodore models, and neither of them yet came with a bubblejet printer, otherwise the font would have been blue and petered out halfway down the page.

The meticulous and institutional paragraph numbering system would have been beyond the wit of any undergraduate, and is clearly the work of a serial civil servant. Attention has also been drawn to the mention of 'translation cards' in section 1.9.3, which would only be required by an army attempting to converse with people from the Isle of Wight. The document is almost certainly genuine.

Almost three decades after the Falklands War, the very notion of anyone invading the Isle of Wight seems absurd and even, much like the island itself, a bit quaint.

Opposite: Despite its great age and terrible typeface, the document 'Operation Free Ventnor' remains strangely relevant and compelling even three decades on.

```
1.3 METHODS OF ATTACK

        1.3.1 Covert assault
                1.3.1.1 Ferry and hovercraft services
                1.3.1.2 Private vessels
                1.3.1.3 By air
                1.3.1.4 The Isle of Wight Festival
        1.3.2 Overt assault
                1.3.2.1 Amphibious assault
                1.3.2.2 Air assault
                1.3.2.3 Movement on the island

    1.4 POTENTIAL RESISTANCE

        1.4.1. Military resistance
                1.4.1.2 Island-based forces
                1.4.1.2 Secondary forces
                1.4.1.3 Off-island forces
```

At the same time, it might not be such a daft idea.

As potential island paradises go, Wight scores quite highly next to, say, anything in the Bermudas or off the coast of Scotland. With its benign climate, celebrated agricultural fertility, excellent ice cream and numerous B&B establishments, it would suit perfectly a committed group of idealists bent on establishing a utopian societal model. With a current population of around 140,000 and a circumference of under sixty miles, it would be very manageable compared with, say, the Isle of Man, which is roughly half as big again and suffers the noise and disruption of two major annual motorcycle meetings[2] and even has a capital named after an old bike.

The Isle of Wight is also a lot more convenient, being no more than three miles from the mainland of Britain, which makes it,

2. The Isle of Man TT and the Manx GP

154

in terms of territorial ambition, the equivalent of camping in the garden but being able to use the lavvy in the house.

Furthermore, the residents of the Isle of Wight may not be as averse to occupation as might be imagined. Regarded by many as a part of both Hampshire and a bygone age, the island is actually its own county, with its own administration. It even has its own joke – what's brown and comes steaming out of Cowes? The Isle of Wight ferry. Unfortunately, it doesn't work in print.

Cartographic convention leads us to think of the Isle of Wight as a small island off the coast of Britain, but to the people who

THE ISLE OF WIGHT for SUNSHINE. SCENERY & SPORT

live there the relationship between the two landmasses is the obverse of this; that is, Great Britain is a large island spoiling the view from Wight's otherwise idyllic northern shores. Many of the island's folk resent being yoked to perfidious Albion like some irrelevant coda to geography. The residents of the Isle of Wight do not harbour a secret ambition to live on the mainland; they harbour a massive yacht moored in Cowes and are delivering a collective Agincourt Salute to the rest of us and our stultifying conventions.

They do, in fact, enjoy a history of embracing free-thinking radicalism. This may sound surprising for a place that hosts a website called 'Isle of Wight Nostalgia', but which few people can distinguish from the regular tourist board offering. Nevertheless, the island's advocates have included, among others, Charles Dickens, the artist J.M.W. Turner, Lewis Carroll and Queen Victoria, who died on the island in 1901 at Osborne House, along with any pretence of further social or technological advancement. In 1642, during the English Civil War, the Isle of

There's not much to grumble about on the Isle of Wight, except perhaps its alarming proximity to the Third World.

Wight fell willingly to the insurgent parliamentarians with the firing of a single symbolic shot. As early as 1548 it boasted of having 'no hooded priests, no lawyers, no wolves, no foxes'. The Isle of Wight claims to be home to Britain's first concrete house, built in 1852, although they still don't like that sort of thing.

But the best reason for invading the Isle of Wight is that they definitely won't be expecting it. As with any island, this other Eden's other Eden has suffered its fair share of unwanted tourists, including the Danes, who raided the place regularly in the early years of the second millennium. King Ethelred the Unready spent Christmas on Wight in 1013 with an old battleaxe.

The nearest Wight has come to true occupation was during the French assault of 1545. In an attempt to outflank the all-powerful English navy, the French landed a total of around 3000 troops at

Queen Victoria, despite being Empress of most of the world, liked Cowes best.

1.0 ATTACK

To consider the challenges implicit in taking control of the Isle of Wight by force, through the use of either covert infiltration or overt assault, with reference to resistance, infrastructure, intelligence gathering and priority targets.

1.1.2 Natural defences

The terrain of the island offers few natural lines of defence. The partially tidal river Medina runs inland from the north coast at Cowes to Newport. It is unbridged and wide enough to present a serious obstacle to forces attempting to travel from east to west, but it can be outflanked by going south of Newport.

Further west the Newtown river and its subsidiaries would hinder movement near the coast, but this is in an underpopulated and strategically unimportant part of the island.

A range of low hills runs across the centre of the island, but these will present few obstacles for a determined and mobile attacking force.

Whitecliff Bay and Bonchurch, the objective being to attack the coastal defences from inland, rather like T.E. Lawrence would at Aqaba in World War I. The French fought their way to Sandown, where they were confronted by a locally raised army of hardy caulkheads.[3]

Both sides suffered heavily in the ensuing battle, and contemporary sources are remarkably reticent about identifying an actual victor. But it must be acknowledged that the island never became known as l'île de Blanc, even with 'blanc' spelled in a slightly funny way, and that the French withdrew soon afterwards. Even today, the croissant is not universally accepted in Sandown.

There have been other intrusions, notably the 1968 bombing of Ventnor by radio-controlled Stukas during the making of *Battle of Britain*, but since the defeat of the Armada in 1588 the Isle of Wight has generally felt safe from what Shakespeare called 'the envy of less happy lands'. But they might be forgetting the big one just a few miles across the silver sea from Yarmouth: England.

Here, then, and drawing heavily on some of the content of the original 1981 document, is an outline plan for an invasion of the Isle of Wight by a force of around two hundred disaffected Britons

---

3. A local sobriquet for people who have lived on the island for many generations. It refers to the caulk used between the timbers of clinker-built boats.

intent on establishing an anarcho-liberal collective. The strategy involves initial shock and awe followed by a period of winning hearts and minds, after which the residents of this delightful demi-paradise will surely join the invaders in establishing autonomy and independence and move forward to a broad sunlit upland, perhaps stopping off for tea and a sticky bun on the way.

OVERVIEW

The Isle of Wight is approximately twenty-three miles in length and a maximum of thirteen miles in width, and is often described optimistically by the locals as 'diamond-shaped'. It has an area of

Above: the failed French attack of 1545. Right: the failed Luftwaffe/United Artists attack of 1940/1968.

148 square miles and a resident population of around 140,000, increasing by up to 25 per cent in the tourist season.

It is separated from Hampshire by the Solent, the remainder of the island being surrounded by the English Channel. Its principal towns are Bembridge, Cowes, Freshwater, Newport,

Ryde, Sandown, Shanklin and Ventnor. Newport is effectively the capital, and the priority objective of an assault.

The island is notoriously difficult to defend, as the locals may be about to find out. Being a small place, the Isle of Wight suffers from a disproportionately long circumference in comparison with its overall area. Its coastline is completely undefended and not systematically patrolled, and although it features several ranges of tall cliffs it also has an abundance of open, sandy beaches well

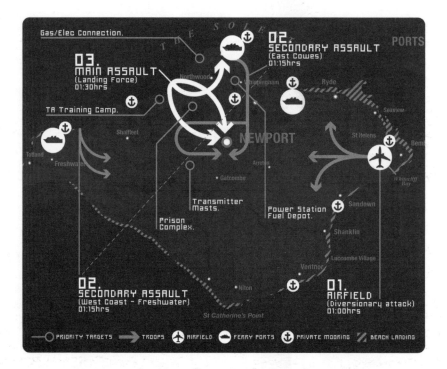

Suggested strategy for a combined shock and awe/covert assault on the unwitting island paradise of Wight.

1.3.2.2 Air assault

The island's gentle topography and large areas of agricultural land also make it vulnerable to air assault through the landing of troops and supplies by parachute, gliders or the use of helicopters in an 'air cavalry' role.

Alternatively, the airfield at Bembridge could be used to launch a surprise attack on the east of the island. The 2750 runway is just 250 feet short of the official minimum landing distance required by a C130 Hercules transport aircraft.

1.4.4. Other risk factors

The island is also home to the largest prison in the UK, HMP Prison Parkhurst, a combined Category B/Category C prison complex north-west of Newport. This currently houses 1700 adult male prisoners, including sexual offenders segregated for their own protection. The facility also has a staff of around 500 prison officers and support workers.

Freed prisoners could form the basis of a resistance movement – or could be used to augment attacking forces or to distract police responses.

suited to late-evening summer walks with someone special or simply as a place to sit and contemplate the mystery and wonder of creation. They are also ideal for amphibious assault in shallow-bottomed vessels.

Indeed, these beaches are regularly used by the Territorial Army to practise landings. However, they do not appear to practise defence *against* amphibious landings. This may be an oversight.

As well as the beaches, the Isle of Wight benefits from excellent public transport links with the mainland, including hovercraft and ferry services to Yarmouth, Cowes and Fishbourne. The 'Puffin' ferries operating out of Lymington could, by themselves, be used to transfer substantial volumes of personnel and ordnance to the island, although it would take a number of trips, as they're quite small. 'Puffin' is not part of the language of aggression and would not arouse suspicion.

There are no customs checks on the Isle of Wight and little in the way of security screening, meaning the invading force will not

be frustrated by the requirement to remove their shoes or place all their hair-care products in a transparent plastic bag before advancing on Newport.

Once ashore, the occupying forces will discover an excellent modern road network and an atrophied but efficient 8.5-mile railway running from Ryde to Shanklin. In addition, there is a much better 'heritage' steam railway operating between Smallbrook Junction and Wootton. Neither of these places are important objectives but the trains are rather charming, and the invading army's figurehead can ensure himself a positive entry in the history books by making them run on time.

A Puffin Ferry, seen here camouflaged as a pleasure vessel.

There is a reliable bus service between Cowes and Newport and bicycles can be hired from a number of places. Troops using these should beware cheese wires stretched across the road by the Resistance.

It should be noted that the very attributes that make the Isle of Wight so easy to invade will also be exploited by Her Majesty's armed forces when they come to retake it. This is why the hearts-and-minds phase of the operation is important in persuading the whole populace to form a unified front against interference. Unlike Galtieri, you will not have the bargaining chip of the Falklands to lay on the table, unless you are reading this as the head of a resurgent South American junta and things are much more serious than we thought.

The island's 'heritage' railway doesn't really go where you want to be.

MAIN OBJECTIVES

In the interest of campaigning a relatively bloodless coup, the principal aim of the invading force should be to take control of those institutions through which the islanders can be persuaded to embrace the new ideology during the 'hearts-and-minds' phase. In addition, basic utilities must be secured and defended against terrorism and sabotage.

The island is administered by a typical unitary local authority with responsibility for everything from education and parking facilities to lesbian outreach workers. Its headquarters are in the conveniently named County Hall in Newport. This is undefended and easy to find using signposts or a local map from one of Wight's six helpful tourist information centres. It has a large car park that, judging from the aerial reconnaissance picture, is largely empty. This could therefore also function as a handy mustering point for assault vehicles. It's pay and display, but only on the weekends. The headquarters of the Isle of Wight's 208-strong police force is also in Newport, conveniently sited opposite the council building, allowing attacking forces to use the same car park and possibly split petrol costs. The fire brigade and the general hospital are in Newport, too, as is its radio station (Isle of Wight Radio, 107.0 and 102.0 MHz) and the offices of the *Isle of Wight County Press* newspaper.

CAR PARK HERE

The island is not entirely self-sufficient in water and relies on the mainland, so the Wight end of the pipes at Gurnard must be protected. Failing this, the island's growing number of upmarket restaurants and gastropubs will be able to supply a huge volume of bottled sparkling water for non-potable tasks such as showering and car washing.

Efforts should be made to secure the island's electricity generating plant at Cowes. Usually, this is used only to supplement the mains undersea cable running from the mainland, and is operated automatically. However, it has a staff of three who should be made to tell you what all the buttons do, at gunpoint. It is fuelled by light oil tanks replenished from the mainland, and this line of supply must be kept open by ensuring the safe passage of convoys, as on Malta from 1941–2.

Newport's central car park, rendevous point for invaders on a budget.

1.6 SUGGESTED INVASION STRATEGIES

The concentration of high-value targets around Cowes and
Newport makes both the priority for an attacking force,
although assaults on other areas of the island should be
considered for their diversionary value.

1.6.1.3 Diversionary operations

A secondary force, conceivably using a different cover
story, could land or move covertly to another location on
the island where it could be used to decoy police armed
response units or to otherwise create confusion.
The most obvious areas for such an attack to target would be
the east or west of the island

The output of this station can be augmented by the waste-to-
energy station at Newport, fuelled by unwanted postcards from
the imperialist era and books titled *Cowes As It Was*.[4]

THE ATTACK

The invading force should be divided into two: one small and
highly mobile unit to mount a swift amphibious assault to seize
principal objectives in Newport and Cowes, and a larger one
landing covertly to secure the island.

The advantage of the overt beach landings is that they would make
it clear to the residents that they were actually being invaded, rather
than merely visited. This would also concentrate the activity of
potential resistance, making it easier to identify and eliminate.

The most obvious place for a full-scale assault is the beaches of
the north coast, from which flanking manoeuvres could be made
on Newport and Cowes. Consideration should be given to a
diversionary airborne raid on the airport at Bembridge, disguised
as a 'fly out' by light aircraft enthusiasts from clubs in the south-
east of England. The covert attack would utilise the island's

4. Is

excellent transport links with the mainland as a means of landing heavy equipment and large numbers of troops. Even so, a degree of subterfuge will be required.

One tactic may be to pose as 'war re-enactors'. This is a popular pastime in the UK in which frustrated middle-aged men dress up as Allied and Axis forces and restage famous engagements from World War II, often drawing a small crowd of bemused onlookers. Since authenticity is the bedrock of this hobby, a large number of functioning period arms will be required,

Empty look-out deck chairs reveal just how complacent the islanders have become about the threat of invasion. The other bloke is merely a bird watcher.

along with live ammunition. By this means it should be possible to bring a Sherman or similar tank to the island. Sadness rather than suspicion will be invoked.

The covert force could also arrive under the pretence of using the Isle of Wight as a location for shooting a war film, especially as parts of it could pass for Cambodia. This would also mean that convincing-looking ordnance could be transferred brazenly to the island and would have the additional advantage of allowing more modern equipment to be used.

The disadvantage of the 'war film' approach is that a certain portion of the force would have to be disguised as film crew, with dummy

War re-enactors trying to pretend they are involved in a 'harmless hobby'.

Although technically part of the strategy for maintaining control of the island (see 'Defensive strategies', Section 2.4), it will nevertheless be necessary to consider the creation of propaganda before the invasion is launched.

Well-prepared propaganda materials can serve to intimidate or confuse the local population, or alternatively to create a positive desire for 'liberation' from the forces of British oppression. Any such propaganda materials, including posters, pamphlets or pre-recorded broadcasts to be transmitted from the island's radio station, should be prepared well in advance of the invasion, although with due regard to security considerations (i.e., don't use any copy shop in the Woking area).

A single, well-led platoon could carry out a covert attack on the island with reasonable expectation of success, provided its sections were capable of acting under individual direction.

This would consist of:

```
1x OC
1x platoon sergeant/senior NCO
1x radio operator
3x 8-man sections, each under the control of a
corporal.
(From the point of view of covert operations, each
section could be split to create two four-man
cells.)
```

Forces would have to be split between Cowes and Newport, with an operational HQ likely established in County Hall and a single section (or half section) sent to capture outlying objectives.

cameras, headphones, sound booms, fashionable puffer jackets and an inconceivable number of belt-mounted multi-tools. However, since during times of conflict most people in Britain rush to join the media, the deceit would soon start to sustain itself.

An alternative strategy might be to use the population influx caused by the Isle of Wight Music Festival in June to move a significant army on to the island. Troops, suitably briefed in

Supposed film crew. The camera is actually a bazooka.

2.1.1.2 Air assault

The Isle of Wight is also very susceptible to attack from the air. The airfield at Bembridge could be captured by a raiding party and then used to fly in troops and supplies, while the island's agricultural centre would be ideal for landing troops and armament by parachute. It would also be possible to ferry an attacking force from a forward operating base on the mainland using helicopters in an 'air cavalry' role.

Targets associated with the post-liberation military power on the island would be extremely vulnerable to direct attack from the air using guided ordnance.

Guarding against any of these risks would require the sourcing, movement and installation of an advanced anti-aircraft defence system.

the use of meaningless left-wing argot, could be disguised as counter-cultural elements such as hippies, ravers and social democrats. Supplies could be smuggled ashore in a fleet of converted coaches, fume-belching VW transporters and old ambulances bearing crudely applied peace symbols.

POTENTIAL RESISTANCE

The Isle of Wight's military complacency means that a well-planned invasion should encounter only limited resistance. It has no fixed defences, no air force, no anti-aircraft capability and no navy.

The only conventional military presence of note is a single Territorial Army Unit, based at Newport. This is likely to have access to modern side arms such as the SA80 rifle and 9mm Browning pistol, but by timing the invasion to miss the unit's weekly drill – Wednesday 19.30 to 21.30 according to its website – it should be possible to catch them off guard.

Harmless hippy or dangerous insurgent?

The island also possesses a military training area, Jersey Camp, near Newtown, which is part of the Cadets Association and used by the Army Cadet Force, the Sea Cadet Corps and the Air Training Corps. However, based on the author's experience of the ATC, the worst the invaders can expect is some excellent barrack-square drill in ill-fitting second-hand uniforms.

Of more concern is the Isle of Wight's tactical police firearms capability, typically two armed blokes in a Volvo estate. They will not only have modern weapons but also effective body armour. Since they combine firearms duties with general traffic policing, it may be possible to effectively neutralise them with a choreographed minor road accident involving a broken wing mirror in a remote part of the island. The danger is that this will instigate the closure of the entire road system.

There is a further danger that the civilian population will form its own defence force, in the style of the Reich's *Volksstrum*. The Isle of Wight is popular with retired colonels and naval officers, whose knowledge of military tactics will

Dangerous old colonel.

2.1.2.1 High Down rocket testing site

The Isle of Wight has a decommissioned rocket test-firing range. This was created as part of the development programme for the 'Black Knight' and 'Black Arrow' rocket motors that were created to power British ballistic missiles in the 1950s and '60s. The facility was active from 1956-1971 and parts of its concrete structure are still substantially intact, including underground rooms used for testing rocket engines. It is located at The Needles at the far west of the island.

With some considerable work - possibly involving the use of prisoners from one of the proposed labour battalions - and with the need to find vintage rockets and enough kerosene/peroxide to fuel them on - it would be possible to turn The Needles into a missile base capable of deterring attack by targeting Lymington, Christchurch or even the eastern suburbs of Bournemouth.

be second only to their understanding of the damaging effects of greenfly. They may be deployed to frustrate the movement of invading troops with lengthy expositions about the problems generated by bloody tourists.

The Isle of Wight has a large and successful gun club, based at Godshill. It specialises in sporting shotguns but also caters for target pistol enthusiasts, who will be good, presumably. It must also be assumed that, as with other parts of the UK, the island will have its fair share of unlicensed and unregistered firearms, although their owners, being the sort of people who keep an illegal firearm, are more likely to join in.

DEFENCE STRATEGIES

It should be recognised by any occupying force that the Isle of Wight will be extremely difficult to defend against the diminished, but still considerable, might of Her Majesty's armed forces.

Even if the freshly divorced Great Britain decided against a full-scale counter-attack, it would be relatively easy to lay siege to the Isle of Wight. Despite agricultural fertility and the production of award-winning garlic (which is actually exported to France), Wight cannot expect to remain self-sufficient in energy and food for more than a few weeks. Alarmingly, from the point of view of the ruling elite of the new administrative order, there is as yet no branch of Waitrose and only one Marks & Spencer.

Consideration should therefore be given to establishing diplomatic means of defence, for example by inviting rogue states

Positions of the UK's main military bases. Having seen this, it's tempting to think that the Isle of Skye would have been a better idea.

After the island has been liberated it will be necessary to establish a mechanism to administer it - referred to here as a Command Committee - with broad powers to exercise control over the existing population and to regulate the affairs of the newly independent Isle of Wight.

2.2.1 TRANSPORT LINKS
It is vital for attacking forces to take control of all transport links, both on the island and between the island and the mainland during the liberation.
This is necessary to prevent resistance elements from coalescing or being reinforced. But also - to follow the example of the erstwhile DDR - to prevent a large part of the island's population from attempting to escape.

2.2.3.3 Control of information
Controlling the access of information will be of paramount importance to winning the propaganda war.

such as Iran, North Korea and France to establish military bases on the island.

Indeed, the island's location in close proximity to one of the most densely populated and conservative-voting parts of the UK mainland mean that it might be possible to invoke the Cold War doctrine of MAD, or Mutually Assured Destruction.

This would involve using diplomatic channels, reinforced by a strong suggestion of widespread insanity on the island, to create fear that any counter-attack would immediately trigger the deployment of a weapon so terrible that the destruction of Wight itself, and most of Hampshire, would be inevitable.

A biological weapon or 'dirty bomb' could be constructed using small quantities of plutonium-238, curium-244 or strontium-90 harvested from newly resident yacht-owning Russian gangsters. The Isle of Wight's prevailing south-westerly winds mean that any contamination released would ultimately make its way to London.

More humanely, the island could be defended by the untried tactic of 'TV ransom'. The Isle of Wight's greatest resource, apart

from the award-winning garlic and world-class carbon-fibre structures, is undoubtedly the fact that TV signals for a large part of the south of England are broadcast from its transmission towers at Rowbridge and Chillerton Down. The new administration could threaten to replace existing broadcasts with French home shopping channels if any attempt was made to retake the island.

Perhaps the riskiest defence strategy would involve discouraging attack by deliberately reducing the Isle of Wight to the level of bestial anarchy through brainwashing and propaganda vilifying certain elements of society, a policy that has served Alabama for two centuries. The downside to this audacious strategy would be a considerable diminution in the high quality of life currently enjoyed by everyone on the Isle of Wight, and the strong possibility of dying in a cannibalistic holocaust.

WINNING HEARTS AND MINDS

As will be clear by now, occupation of the Isle of Wight will only be possible with the consent and cooperation of the existing population. Hence a hearts-and-minds initiative will be essential.

Liberation of the island could be promoted as an attempt to save it from the hedonistic, sinful aspirations of modern Britain, and to

The full horror of French daytime TV in production. Oh, the humanity!

Monaco

return it to the moral certitude of a gentler age. Its faded grandeur
as a tourist destination makes a 'back-to-basics' manifesto based
on a return to 1950s values very appealing and, let's be honest,
easy to instigate. The island would then become financially solvent
through the money spent by nostalgic *Daily Mail* readers.

The Isle of Wight is currently denied the 'tax break' status afforded
other similarly sized British sovereign territories such as the
Channel Islands and the Isle of Man, a situation that is known to
cause resentment among its wealthier residents. Rectification of this
could turn the Isle of Wight into the Monaco of the British Isles,
i.e., an overpriced concrete shithole full of obnoxious millionaires.

A declaration of independence should be made as soon as
possible, promising freedom and autonomy for Wightans in
vague language, preferably from the steps of the County Hall
in Newport. Media coverage could be assured by enlisting the
support of a sympathetic celebrity such as Joanna Lumley. Failing
that, media coverage could be assured by enlisting the support
of an unprincipled celebrity such as Simon Cowell, and then
publicly executing him in front of a baying and blood-crazed
mob. Space should be found for other countries to establish
embassies in central Newport. The area between Yates's Wine
Lodge and the Carphone Warehouse on High Street is ideal.

To prevent any political dissent from coalescing, and to project a positive image of life on the liberated island, serious consideration should be given to the appointment of a well-loved figurehead president. The most obvious candidate would be Mark King, former bassist with the eighties electro-funk fusion beat combo Level 42, a native of the island. King could be persuaded to return with the promise of a palace in Cowes and the chance to teach his pioneering 'slap bass' technique to all residents.

This could then be used as an effective shibboleth. Anyone claiming to be part of the New Order but unable to play along to 'Running in the Family' would be summarily executed.

HOW TO SURRENDER:

Contact the Isle of Wight constabulary

Queen Victoria is dead. Long live Mark King, King of Cowes.

chapter SEVEN

Our imagined mate Bob could be disposed of in a fortifying pot-based dehydrated meal supplement. It's what he would have wanted.

Whichever way you look at it, death, like coming to the end of a Pot Noodle, leaves us with a simple issue of disposal. Once, we would put the pot in the bin, and that would be that. Now we might have to put it in a particular bin, so that it can be turned into another pot.

Bear with me on this.

Back in the Victorian era, a man's death meant simply that a body had to be buried. Today, though, the options regarding the fate of one's mortal remains are surprisingly extensive and, as with aluminium beer cans and plastic bags, a culture of recycling and reuse has emerged.

In extreme cases, you can bequeath your corpse to a radical art exhibition and enjoy an extra decade or so flashing your private parts at shocked voyeurs. More traditionally, you can donate your body to medical science, ensuring that a future generation of practitioners can learn vital surgical techniques before practising on someone still living. If you've ever undergone an operation, you should be thankful that the skill and dexterity displayed in putting you back together was in part the result of someone's generosity in death.

Perhaps most significantly, we have the well-established Donor Card scheme, a once-thorny matter clouded by ethical and moral debate but now so widely accepted that it is possible to register as an organ donor while applying online to join the Boots Advantage loyalty points scheme. By simply filling out an application for a handy wallet-friendly card you can elect to donate, in the event of your untimely demise, any or everything, from your heart to the cornea of an eye to skin tissue, to help someone else live. Major organ donation alone is reckoned to save around three thousand lives a year in Britain, and the figure is rising as the science of transplanting develops apace.

It's all good heart-warming stuff, especially if yours used to belong to someone else. But there is still one very dark taboo regarding bodily donation. As yet there is no card bearing the legend 'I would like to help someone eat after my death'. Why is not entirely clear. You could give the gift of lunch.

Everyone is dimly aware that, in times of desperation, people will eat each other. There are numerous well-documented instances of this throughout history, most famously the crash of Uruguayan Air flight 571 in the Andes in 1972. The survivors, marooned for seventy-two days, eventually resorted to eating the flesh of those who had died in the crash.

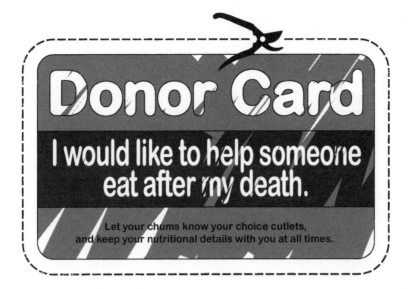

Further back, the Donner Party, a particularly inept group of American pioneers who went west in 1846 but ended up stranded in the Sierra Nevada for the winter, sustained itself with the bodies of the deceased. Their legacy of culinary pragmatism lives on in the so-called 'doner kebab', an emergency-only foodstuff formed from meat of indeterminate origin.

Accounts from people who have been forced to consume their own kind are inevitably peppered, ho-ho, with moralistic caveats. It is never going to be easy to eat someone, and it should not be attempted except as an absolute last resort,[1] but our natural reticence would at least be eased if people carried cards acknowledging their willingness to be treated as a basic provision in times of dire need. Over 17 million UK residents have declared, through the donor scheme, that they would be happy for someone else to make use of their liver in the accepted role of a liver. All that is required is to be happy that it might be used more like a pâté.

1 Lawyers, again.

The proposed human foodstuffs Donor Card. Please insert your own tasteless kebab jokes here.

'A little like an empty box in your attic'

184

Is this really that difficult? We know, from the work of René Descartes,[2] that we do not exist as the body, but rather as the mind, and it follows that when the mind has fled, the body remains as nothing more than a hollow vessel.

Consider the typical scenario of a plane crash in a remote area. You have survived, but your old mate of many years standing was not so lucky. Surely, if you could ask him, he would say that he wouldn't want you to perish too, merely for want of sustenance. His mortal, corporal form is nothing more than a former host to his departed soul, and viewed in that way is a little like an empty box in your attic, but with higher calorific value. You have to eat something, and to eat the anonymous corpse of a business executive from the posh seats at the front of the crash site would be an insult, frankly.

You might like to bolster yourself with the knowledge that what you are about to do is not technically cannibalism. Cannibalism requires the premeditated slaughter of a fellow human being with the aim of eating him. The scientific term for what is being proposed here is 'intraspecific necrophagy', which somehow doesn't sound as bad.

One day, in the future, you will look back with fondness on the great times you shared with the old mucker. You will perhaps

2 *Meditations on First Philosophy*, 1641

treasure some small memento of his life: a photograph, a trinket, that bottle opener he gave you. But only if you survive. In the short term, you'll be better off celebrating his life by remembering him as a tasty and life-sustaining snack item.

Basic NUTRITIONAL information

Precise data on the calorific value of human meat is, understandably, not really available.

William Seabrook, a barking-mad occultist who claimed to have eaten human whilst living with an openly cannibalistic tribe in West Africa during the 1930s, noted only that the taste was that of 'mild, good meat with…no sharply defined or highly characteristic taste such as, for instance, goat, high game and pork have'. But of its contribution to a balanced daily intake, or of the presence of omega-3 polyunsaturated fatty acids, he left no record.

It doesn't help that while, for example, beef cattle are selectively bred and fed, human beings are essentially free-range and extremely variable, rather like the knobbly carrots from the farmers' market.

What we do know is that, like all the red varieties, human meat is energy dense. Different parts of the body will have different values according to the relative percentages of fat and muscle (i.e., protein). Legs and arms will generally be well developed but, and especially if your old chum was a bit of a slob, buttocks and belly less so.

Let's assume, reasonably, that human is roughly equivalent to beef or pork in terms of energy value. That means between 200 and 400 calories per 100 grams.

Of course, only a limited percentage of the carcass can actually be eaten. For a fully prepared cow, from which every effort to extract food and even high-street quarter pounders has been made, the 'yield' is typically 60 per cent of the dead weight.

It will be lower for a human. For starters, ho-ho again, we're less fleshy: we have proportionally more bone (the downside of walking upright), bigger brains and so on. We should also assume that things like offal are off-limits, unless you're French. In short, only 30 per cent of a thirteen-stone bloke is likely to be 'easily' edible. That means around twenty-four kilograms of meat, with an estimated mean total calorific value of 72,000.

As an adult male requires 2500 calories a day, your departed drinking companion has the potential to sustain you for 28.8 days. But since you're only going to tuck into Bob when you're desperate, and you're never likely to say 'Oh, I know I shouldn't, but I'll just have a bit more', we can double that. He can probably keep you alive for two months.

Not bad for someone who probably only owed you a curry.

CUTS *of* MATE

As we have seen, muscle makes the best meat and, depending on his former lifestyle to an extent, your chum's body is similar to the carcass of a pig when it comes to selecting the best bits. Muscle is predominantly located in the arms and legs and at the front and back of the chest.

The main, and most fortuitous, advantage of the human is that it provides those bulky arms and legs. This is handy, because it means anyone without the skills, tools and stomach required for a proper butchery job can simply lop one off and treat it as a traditional roasting joint.

The main advantage of the pig is that you weren't at school with it, so there's no emotional attachment.

But to the amateur, the human's big bones are a help because, as Delia has pointed out many times,[3] they help to distribute heat evenly throughout the meat. But let's not get bogged down in gastronomy. We're looking at starvation rations here, not trying to revive the fortunes of a crap local pub through food poncery.

3 The lawyers would like me to make quite clear that Delia has never pointed this out to me in person and indeed not to anyone in the context of cooking people.

A comparison between the pig and the human is not as revealing as I first thought when I suggested these diagrams.

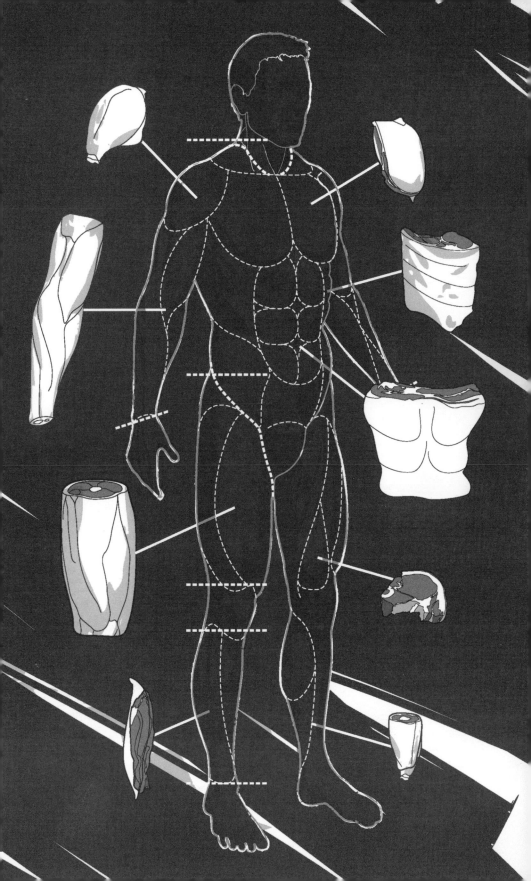

Simple BUTCHERY

A real butcher would use a meat saw to remove an arm or a leg, but as this will be unavailable you will have to soldier on with a sharp knife. Sadly, in the modern world your Swiss Army penknife will be in your checked-in luggage, so you will have to rummage through the wreckage in the hope that your bag was put on the right aeroplane. Failing this, rudimentary blades can be fashioned from broken glass, as they were by the Andes survivors.

A real butcher would probably also remove the head if this were a bullock. This is not necessary here, but it might be a good idea to cover it in order to avoid being distracted by that remonstrative deadpan stare that your pal used to reserve for your ill-judged one-liners down the pub.

Remove the limb from the torso by cutting through the connective tissues to the bone, and then finish the job with a heavy blow from a rock or a piece of aeroplane. Remove the hands and feet, as this will greatly reduce the impression that you are eating a person. In this respect presentation remains important.

You will now need to skin the arm or leg. This is the most grizzly task required of you, but once done will leave the limb largely unidentifiable as a part of someone you once knew. Basically, you will have to peel the skin off as you might the skin of a giant orange, albeit one of such an unusual shape that it would have featured on *That's Life!* Human skin is tough, so you may have to work it off in patches, using your blade to separate the dermis and epidermis from the quality stuff underneath.

You now have your roasting joint. But you could go further. Cutting around the knee or elbow and then slicing along the length of the bone will leave you with a lump of boneless meat that could be chopped into steaks. Alternatively, it could be sliced lengthways to produce a poor imitation of bacon.

All things considered, 'on the bone' is probably best.

PRESERVING *Meat* in *Hostile* CLIMATES

It is only relatively recently that society has mastered the science of storing fresh meat. This is why, in earlier times, people kept live animals and slaughtered them only when they were ready to be eaten, whereas now we have refrigeration.

In cold climates it's not such an issue. If the prevailing temperature is at or below zero, then it will be a relatively simple matter to build a cold store to protect your supplies from marauding scavengers. Note that you should perform the basic butchery before storage because, as anyone who has ever liberated a pack of sausages from the icebox will know, dividing up frozen meat is nigh-on impossible.

If you have read the instruction book that came with your freezer – few have – you should know that although low temperatures greatly reduce the rate of decay, they don't arrest it entirely. Therefore, if you anticipate a long wait for rescue it may be worth considering some of the preservation methods for hot climates, just to be on the safe side.

Hot climates present many more problems. Your mate will start to putrefy within a matter of hours. Within half a day insects will have moved in and visible decomposition will occur within a few days. Black putrefaction will set in before a week is out and in tropical climates a corpse can be reduced to bones in as little as ten days.

Dry-curing is probably the simplest way to preserve meat, although it does require a great deal of salt, which means opening thousands of those airline sachets, half the contents of which will land on your trousers anyway. This will need to be done as soon as possible, leaving you little time to wrestle with the moral maze leading to the dismemberment of your old china plate.

Take your piece of meat and rub salt into it, as deeply and evenly as the snow in the Wenceslas carol and leaving no part exposed. Place the meat in a sealed container (there will be plenty of these in the aeroplane's galley) and leave it in the coolest place you can find. Swift and decisive action after the crash will mean you can still use buckets of ice and chilled bottles of Chardonnay from business class.

Every eighteen to twenty-four hours remove the meat from the box and pour away the liquid that has leached from it. Rub more salt in and return it to the box. Repeat until no more liquid appears – this should take between four and eight days – then rinse the meat in clean water and allow to dry. You should see an even coating of 'pellicle', a waxy protein that looks a bit like mould. The meat should now last several weeks. This technique was used in ancient China, and doesn't seem to have done them any harm.

Wet-curing, as favoured by Danish bacon producers, is a little more complex but quicker and less labour intensive. You will need a non-reactive container such as glass or plastic, as the strong brine involved will cause corrosion of some sort in most common metals. You will also need to build a cold store

A basic cold store improvised from bits of aeroplane, used to store bits of passenger. Remember to separate joints first.

to regulate the temperature of the process to between two and four degrees Celsius. There will be a thermometer in the airline's first-aid kit.

Add two kilograms of salt to twenty litres of water and boil. Cool the resulting brine in the cold store and then add the meat, making sure it is entirely submerged. Leave for between twenty-four hours and four days, then hang in fresh air until dried out. The longer you leave the meat in the brine, the deeper the cure and the more resistant to decay it will be. Well-cured pieces should last for several weeks.

This may not, however, be the most palatable method. As anyone who has fried cheap supermarket own-brand bacon will know, wet-curing can add considerable moisture content to meat, making it difficult to achieve crispiness.

The life of cured meat can be further extended by smoking. It should be fairly easy to construct a smoker from aircraft wreckage – it's really a simple combination of an oven and a smoke cabinet. Sadly, the process will only work if the crash site is abundant with quality smoking fuels, such as wood chips or bark. Seat foam, aviation fuel and in-flight shopping magazines won't work at all.

COOKING

The galley of a modern airliner is designed only for partially reheating prepared food, and is therefore unlikely to yield much in the way of useful equipment for your improvised kitchen. Furthermore, the ovens run on electricity, and now the engines have stopped there's none of that.

Having said that, the crash site should provide plenty in the way of basic seasoning, bottled water and annoyingly short-handled cutlery.

The easiest way to cook small pieces of Bob for one or two diners would be to make a fire, using the aeroplane's fuel as a starter, and then fashion a simple griddle from a piece of aluminium. Select as thick a piece as possible – search around wing roots, undercarriage bays and engine pylons – because this will retain heat like a copper-bottomed pan. Ideally you would need some cooking oil, but fattier bits of meat will effectively baste themselves, as Spam does in a frying pan.

Get the griddle as hot as possible and then, holding the meat with a fork, quickly sear it all around. It can then be fried more slowly, checking with a knife point to ensure it is cooked through. Serve well done.

Boiling is also an attractive option. There is no evidence that cannibals ever boiled their victims alive in a huge comedy tulip-shaped pot while dancing around it in grass clothing, but boiling is a good and safe way of serving up small offcuts and scraps.

Place the meat in a storage bin from the galley, cover with water and position over the fire. Piquancy can be added by throwing in salt 'n' vinegar crisps, Cheesy Wotsits and pretzels from the 'raid the larder' basket on British Airways crashes. With a long boil and very small pieces of meat, it should be possible to create a hearty winter warming soup. Skim the fatty layer from the top and store in an old marmalade jar as stock.

For larger dinner parties you should consider roasting a whole joint. In cold and barren areas this will mean building an oven – basically a heated box – out of aeroplane bits. A storage bin from the galley should be positioned in a sheltered area over a fire made from upholstery, reading matter and the clothing of the deceased. Bear in mind that on modern aircraft seat filling will

Making a simple ground oven, a technique that may have been popular with genuine 19th century cannibals.

be fireproof as a result of the inquiry into the 1985 Manchester air disaster, while on older models it may give off toxic smoke.

In temperate climes a better solution would be a ground oven, a method used by the Maori of New Zealand (where it is known as a '*hangi*') and still favoured by the Scouts. This, allegedly, was a popular technique with real cannibals, although some modern historians claim that all accounts of such things were gross exaggerations designed to feed the bored minds of a sensation-hungry era. The contrary view says that such revisionism is merely bed-wetting liberalism by people keen to foist their ideas of morality on earlier and unrelated cultures.

According to William Mariner, who recorded the activities of Hapai men in his 1827 *Account of the Natives of Tonga Islands*:

> The carcass was laid in a hole in the ground lined with hot stones, a fire having previously been made there for the purpose, but prevented from touching them by small branches of the breadfruit tree. A few other branches were then laid across the back of the carcass, and plenty of banana leaves strewn, or rather heaped, over the whole; upon which, again, a mound of earth was raised so that no steam could escape. By these means, the carcass could very well be cooked in half an hour.

First dig a pit. Cover the bottom of this with rocks or, if they are unavailable, substantial metal sections of the airframe, packing them as tightly together as possible. Pile combustible material on top of this and light it. Branches are ideal, but failing that anything will do including Jet A-1 fuel. The important thing is to let it burn away completely before going further.

If you have done this correctly the rocks will be hot enough to burn your face if you stand over the pit. The bigger the rocks, the greater their heat capacity.

Taking your cue from the Hapai, place a thin layer of sticks or leaves over the rocks. These will create steam and help with the cooking process, and also prevent the meat from being burnt in direct contact with the rocks. Throw in the meat, cover with another layer of sticks or leaves, and then bury under the earth you dug out of the pit in the first place.

Accepted practice says that for well-done meat you should allow thirty minutes per kilogram at gas mark 7. This temperature may be difficult to maintain, and Mariner's claim that a whole carcass could be cooked in half an hour sounds optimistic. Aim for a slow roast for five or six hours.

Remove the meat from the oven, carve as best you can with the pathetic excuse for a knife that airline passengers must endure post 9/11, season with salt and pepper and serve with uneaten salad from First Class. Enjoy.

Author's note

If supplies of your mate become exhausted, or you are too squeamish for this, you may have to eat one of the pre-packed meals from the economy section of the aircraft.

CHAPTER EIGHT

- Save £££s on bomb disposal with this clear, easy-to-follow DIY guide.

- No specialist tools required, although the needle thing is quite hard to find.

- Potentially fatal.

ISBN 123-1-939-194500

1 231939 194501

ames
DIY GUIDES

HOW TO DEFUSE AN UNEXPLODED
WORLD WAR II
GERMAN
BOMB

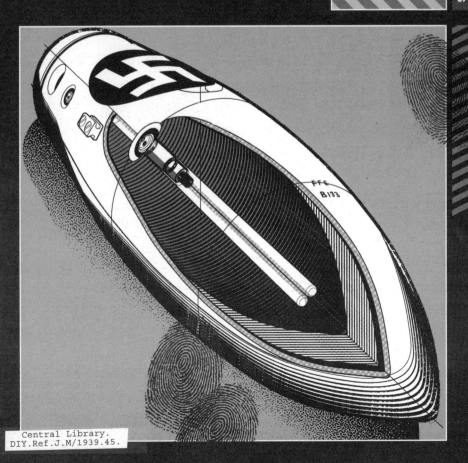

James ®

FFE
B133

'When the British Air Force drops two or three or four thousand kilograms of bombs, then we will in one night drop 150, 230, 300 or 400,000 kilograms. When they declare that they will increase their attacks on our cities, then we will raze their cities to the ground.' (Crowd cheers deliriously)
– ADOLF HITLER, 4 SEPTEMBER 1940

Never in the field of human conflict has so much unadulterated tosh been spoken by one man with bad breath and a silly moustache. Having been incensed by a retaliatory raid by the RAF on Berlin, the first thing the Fuhrer should have done is consult *Das Buch des Beobachters von Flugzeugen*.[1]

The simple statistics he might have learned there are these. Germany's bombers, covertly developed from 'fast airliners' of the mid-1930s, were never intended for what became known as 'strategic bombing'. The Heinkel 111, the mainstay of the Luftwaffe's offensive against Great Britain, could carry 2000kg of bombs; Britain's Avro Lancaster would be able to carry over three times that amount, and they would be deployed in four or five times the number.

1 *The Observer's Book of Aircraft*

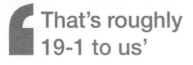
That's roughly
19-1 to us'

Germany dropped under 75,000 tonnes of bombs on Britain during World War II. The British and American air forces between them delivered almost 1.4 million tonnes of high explosives to the Reich. As straightforward score sheets go, that's roughly 19–1 to us and that, as Dr Johnson might have said, is an end on 't.

Except that, and as many old colonels are keen to tell us, the war isn't quite over yet. It is estimated that one in ten of the Luftwaffe bombs dropped on Britain didn't go off for some reason – faulty fuses, incorrect arming, possibly even deliberate sabotage by workers forced into the Reich armaments industry in the occupied countries. Some were found and dealt with at the time, but many were not. Under the streets and pleasant parks of London alone there are over 100 known unexploded bombs, or UXBs, that are considered best left well alone.[2] But there will be more, and, like those Japanese soldiers marooned on Pacific islands, they may not accept that it's all over.

And so, mindless of the fading spectre of the long-vanquished Fuhrer, you happily dig your vegetable plot, the footings for a new garden wall, or the foundations for your extension. And then the sleeping dogs of war are summoned in the terrifying clang of Spear and Jackson's finest clashing with the cold steel of unresolved National Socialist ambition.

2 For example, and rather ironically, there are two in Lambeth Cemetery.

But wait a moment. Let's be realistic. It's been there for a lifetime, so it probably won't go off. Then again, 'probably' is not a useful word in bomb disposal. So on second thoughts, leg it.

As you flee you might like to consider your ill fortune. Unexploded bombs are rarely encountered in domestic excavations, because even the smaller ones tended to bury themselves about twenty feet under the surface. A big 'Satan' 4000 pounder ('pahnder' if you live in the East End and in a film about the Blitz) could penetrate up to sixty feet. This is why contractors for big building works, where deep piles have to be sunk, take the UXB threat very seriously, consult 'UXB risk maps' and make electromagnetic surveys of the site to check for unwanted gifts from Jurgen and Klaus.

On the other hand, bombs have been unearthed during activities as innocent as building a patio in a pub beer garden, so we must all be vigilant.

What is generally accepted by experts in 'UXB Risk Assessment' is that actual bombing was denser than contemporary records suggested, not least because counting bombs during an air raid must have been quite difficult. Obviously, areas such as East London, the Midlands and Hull were prime targets for the Luftwaffe, and on UXB maps they are marked in red (very high

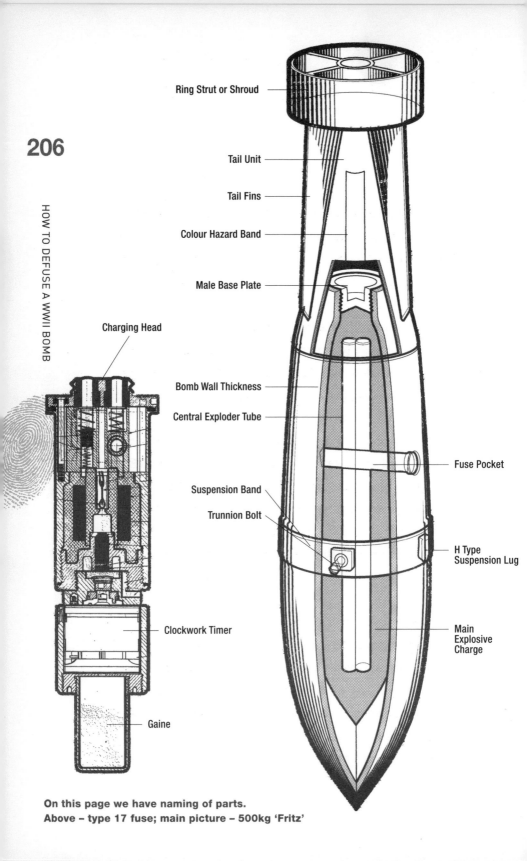

Ring Strut or Shroud

Tail Unit

Tail Fins

Colour Hazard Band

Male Base Plate

Charging Head

Bomb Wall Thickness

Central Exploder Tube

Fuse Pocket

Suspension Band

Trunnion Bolt

H Type
Suspension Lug

Main
Explosive
Charge

Clockwork Timer

Gaine

On this page we have naming of parts.
Above – type 17 fuse; main picture – 500kg 'Fritz'

risk). But at least in these places, the wartime government's efforts to record the fall of bombs provide a few useful pointers. 'Bomb densities' have been calculated – Battersea, to take an extreme case, is rated at 514 bombs per 1000 acres.

You could also just take a look around. This author's house is a post-war building in an otherwise nineteenth-century street. There are several other architectural upstarts at intervals along the road. All this suggests bomb damage.

A German bomber in the early stages of the Blitz – say the Heinkel 111 mentioned above – might typically have carried eight 250kg general purpose *bomben*, which would have been released in quick succession in what is known in bombing circles as a 'stick'. A stick like this clearly worked its way along my road. Now, statistically, there's a fair chance that one of them didn't go off. It may have been dealt with at the time, but it may have gone unnoticed.

Amazingly, it is a simple matter to verify the hazards attendant on jacuzzi building in the garden with an on-line UXB risk map at www.zetica.com. My district has a bomb density of 311 per 1000 acres, and there are three known 'abandoned bombs'[3] within half a mile of the house. All this brings an extra frisson of excitement to any roadworks going on outside the front door.

3 That is, known UXBs that are considered no threat and have been left where they are.

208

But don't imagine that just because you live in the cuds you are safe. Aerial navigation in the 1940s was an inexact science, even for the Germans, who had pioneering but primitive radio-based guidance systems such as Knickebein. Bomber crews became lost, scared, low on fuel or were bounced by John 'Cat's Eyes' Cunningham in his radar-equipped Bristol Beaufighter, and sometimes released their loads at random in the interests of a quick getaway. Dud bombs that fell in open country were less likely to be noticed than those that fell in cities, and what was open country in the mid-1940s might now be a housing estate or the site of a proposed sports centre. So even today, no one is entirely safe from those marauding Nazi thugs.

But back to our bomb, in the garden. There is now really only one option open to you: evacuate the area and move people into the Anderson shelter (or the underground if in London), give them a cup of beef tea, a gramophone and some Vera Lynn records and then, alone and uncheered, stride purposefully and manfully back to the hole to confront the beast. This is what's known in the bomb disposal business as 'the long walk'. According to the Joint Services Conventional Munitions Disposal Wing (JS CMD Wg) the ideal temperament for this is 'barking mad or a stable extrovert'.

Note that the bomb lacks characteristic tail fins. They were made from mild steel or aluminium sheet, and usually broke

away on impact. Their absence rather spoils the comedic bomb-
sticking-out-of-a-hole appearance of the scene, but they can be
reinstated by cartoonists celebrating your exploit in the press.

Dig carefully around the bomb, without subjecting it to shocks
or unnecessary movement, to locate the fuse pocket. On larger
bombs there may be two, so check the whole thing. Our example
bomb is a 1400kg Fritz, a big bugger. On German bombs fuse
pockets were located on the side of the casing rather than in the
nose. The fuse itself is inserted in the pocket and takes the form of
a shiny disc with baffling markings.

Here's how it works, or hopefully doesn't. It is an electrical contact
resistance fuse, or *elektrischer aufschadzunder*. In the base of the
fuse is a one-inch plug of highly explosive penthrite wax, called
a 'gaine'. The gaine is surrounded by a hollow ring of picric acid,
and the remainder of the fuse pocket, leading to the explosives in
the bomb itself, is filled with pellets of the same.

When the bomb was released, a burst of electricity was passed through
the bomb's charging head – a clip-on device inserted in the fuse
when the aircraft was 'bombed up'. This charge was stored in a firing
condenser, ready to trigger the gaine and with it the whole bomb. This
might happen on impact, or it might happen after a delay effected by a
clockwork timer. In your case it hasn't happened at all – yet.

Jason Hill of the JS CMD Wg, our guide for this exercise, the man in the pictures and someone to be trusted on the grounds of the shine on his shoes alone, says, 'You have to give the Germans credit. They were geniuses, evil geniuses. Their stuff was more advanced than ours and it was beautifully made.'

But because the device relies on an electrical capacitor, you should be perfectly safe. The charge would reduce to nothing after a maximum of about forty days, rendering the bomb inert. But should any detractor suggest as much from the safety of the Anderson you should respond thus: the decay of the gaine may have formed highly explosive picric acid crystals in the fuse pocket, and these can still be triggered by shock or friction.

Now you must identify the type of fuse or fuses. The two types that interest us here, and are most likely to be encountered today, are the time delay and the anti-disturbance. The Germans, ultimately doomed to being German, marked everything very clearly, making life easier for the bomb disposal people, such as you. Look for a number stamped in a small circle.

The Type 17 is the delayed action fuse, set in the factory to explode anything between thirty minutes and seventy-four hours after impact, the latter being the supposed limit set under the Geneva Convention. It uses a clockwork timing mechanism in addition to the resistance fuse. This was the type of fuse fitted to the 2000lb bomb found during early work on the London Olympics site in 2008.

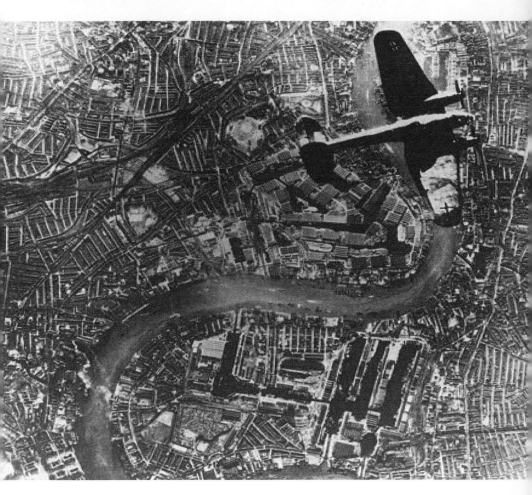

Germans bombing the 2012 London Olympic village in 1940.

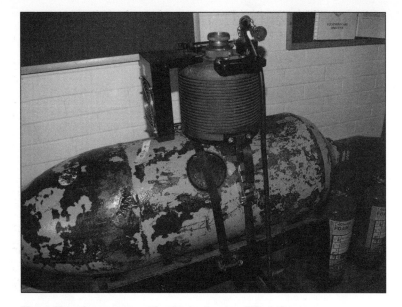

Fig. 1 The electromagnetic clock-stopper. What do you mean you haven't got one?

The Type 50 is the anti-disturbance fuse, using trembler switches to fire the charge if the bomb is moved or struck.

Eventually, the Germans realised that marking their fuses in this way gave our brave bomb disposal boys a vital clue, so they started leaving the case of the Type 17 blank. If you find a blank fuse, it's a Type 17, because this was the only type they *didn't* mark. Clearly, they were never going to win.

So, for the purposes of this demonstration, you have uncovered a Type 17 delay fuse. If you can hear it ticking faintly, you will need a powerful electromagnetic clock-stopper (Fig. 1).

Chances are you don't have one, in which case I would refer you to paragraph six above. In fact, I'll save you the bother. Leg it.

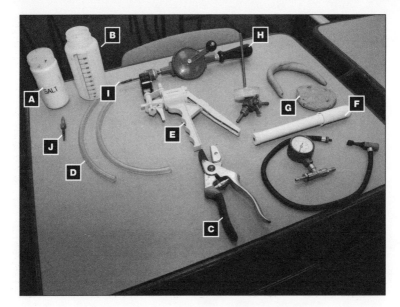

Fig. 2 A typical DIY bomb-disposal kit. Item J, the self-tapping needle, is very difficult to find, except in Bagshot.

All being well, you should now exit your hole and go to B&Q to buy your bomb disposal kit (Fig. 2). It consists of:

A Pot of salt

B Pot of water

C Pair of scissors or secateurs

D Length of plastic tubing

E Hand-operated vacuum pump

F Small bicycle pump

G Lump of putty or plasticine

H Hand drill

I 4mm drill bit

J A self-tapping needle

1. Make up a saturated salt solution (Fig. 3)

Fig. 3 Making up the saturated salt solution in a calm and unhurried manner, while wearing an appropriate jumper.

2. Check the contents of your vacuum pump kit and assemble it (Figs. 4a, 4b).

Figs. 4a, 4b Checking the components of, and then assembling, your vacuum pump kit, in appropriately shiny shoes.

3. Form your putty or plasticine into two pieces – one snake-shaped, the other like a pancake (Figs. 5a, 5b).

Fig. 5a, 5b Shaping the putty or plasticine: pancake-shaped piece (left), snake-shaped piece (right).

4. Check – very important – that the self-tapping needle is clear of obstructions (Fig. 6).

5. This is the trickiest bit. Using the drill and 4mm bit, make a small hole between the outer skin of the fuse and the pocket it sits in. Use a strip of tape wound around the drill

Fig. 6 Look through the needle. Is it clear?

bit to set the depth of the hole at about 6mm. Do this slowly and smoothly, and resist the temptation to get the electric

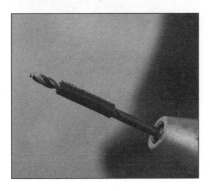

Fig. 7a Using tape to mark the drilling depth at 6mm.

Bosch out of the shed. The picric acid crystals that will have formed in the fuse pocket are sensitive to friction, and you could set off a chain reaction, detonating the whole bomb (Figs. 7a, 7b, 7c).

Figs. 7b, 7c Drilling the hole,
extremely carefully.

6. Assuming the last bit went well, screw the self-tapping
needle into the hole you've just drilled (Fig. 8).

Fig. 8 The self-tapping needle firmly screwed home, carefully.

Figs. 9a, 9b, 9c Forming an airtight seal between the fuse pocket and the bomb casing, using the putty, very carefully.

7. Use the snake-shaped piece of putty or plasticine to make an airtight seal between the rim of the fuse and the bomb casing. Use the pancake-like bit to seal the face of the fuse around the self-tapping needle (Figs. 9a, 9b, 9c).

8. Attach the assembled vacuum pump to the self-tapping needle with the plastic tubing. Pump until the dial shows a vacuum equal to twenty-five inches of mercury (Figs. 10a, 10b, 10c).

Fig. 10a Carefully attaching the plastic tubing.

Fig. 10b, 10c Using the pump to create a vacuum equal to 25 inches of mercury in the fuse pocket, carefully.

9. Using the valve on the pump, allow the salt solution to be drawn into the fuse pocket (Fig. 11).

Fig. 11 Opening the valve to allow the salt solution to flow into the fuse pocket, whilst maintaining a steely gaze.

Fig. 12 Pressurising the fuse pocket using the small bicycle pump. Return the pump to the bicycle afterwards if you survive.

10. Now use the bicycle pump to pressurise the fuse pocket. Pump until salt solution bubbles out of your snake and pancake seal. The fuse is now full of salt water (Fig. 12).

11. Cut the tubing close to the fuse with the scissors or secateurs (Fig. 13).

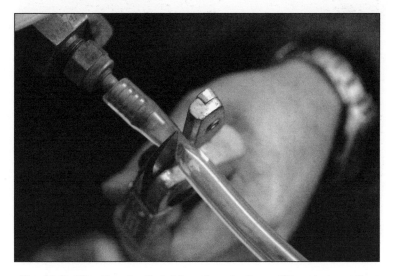

Fig. 13 Cutting the plastic tubing close to the self-tapping needle. Retain long piece of tubing for the next bomb disposal job.

12. Put up a deck chair and sit tight for at least 45 minutes, reading a copy of the *London Illustrated News* or similar. Our man is shown looking at his watch in theatrical fashion.

13. Knock out the fuse. The 'before' and 'after' pictures show the work of the salt solution in gumming up the meticulous clockwork of the Reich war machine (Figs. 15a, 15b).

Figs. 15a, 15b The clockwork mechanism before (left) and after (right) it was disabled with the salt solution.

Figs. 15c, 15d German fuses: the ever-popular Type 17 (left) and the similar 50 YB anti-disturbance version (right).

Keep the disabled fuse in a coat pocket to help illustrate your story in public houses. If your life ended very suddenly at this point it was because the German armourers had also fitted something called a ZUS40 (Figs. 15c, 15d, 15e), a spring-loaded booby trap installed immediately below the regular fuse and designed to set off the bomb when it was removed, thus killing a vital bomb disposal officer. Bad luck. If that didn't happen and you're still with us:

Fig. 15e The ZUS40 booby trap fuse, something you will never be able to admire in reality. So where did this one come from?

Fig. 16 Posing for a photograph with the disabled bomb. Do not strike heroic poses. Appear modest and smile.

14. Pose with safe bomb for picture (Fig. 16).

15. Sound the All Clear and mentally prepare yourself
   for the unqualified adoration of your peers.

AUTHOR'S DISCLAIMER

Do not actually do any of this. This book
is intended for male fantasy entertainment
purposes only. In the unlikely event that you
do discover an unexploded World War II
German bomb, stay well clear of it, evacuate
the neighbourhood and call the boys in.

Ludwig van BEETHOVEN - (1770-1827) - Op.27 No.2

Moonlight SONATA

chapter nine

How to Play the First
Movement* of Beethoven's
Piano Sonata in C-Sharp Minor,
Opus 27, No. 2 *Quasi Una
Fantasia* the 'Moonlight'
with No Previous Experience

* The first bit anyway

Ludwig van BEETHOVEN
(1770-1827)

There is a very good reason why the first movement of the so-called Moonlight Sonata has become one of the most famous pieces in the entire pianoforte canon.

It was dedicated by Beethoven on a particularly bad herr day to his pupil, the Countess Julie Guicciardi, a young woman for whom the tousle-headed tunesmith was suffering an all-consuming, utterly debilitating but ultimately unrequited love. And it shows. This is not so much a piece of music as an annotation of an affair of the heart; the means by which Beethoven exorcised his soul of accumulated lust and despair. 'Even today, two hundred years later, it's ferocity is astonishing,' said the music theorist Charles Rosen.

Countess
Julie
Guicciardi

In fact, some pianists have gone so far as to say that it is possible to play this seminal work convincingly only if you are, in fact, in love, and that the sensitive listener will understand, at a visceral level, the torment of the

performer simply from the tenderness of his phrasing.
When well executed, Opus 27, No.2 is a highly protracted
act of foreplay.

This is precisely why you should learn to play it. Towards the
end of any respectable house party, when the empty boasting
of braggarts and charlatans has been exhausted and the
mood becomes as still as the surface of Lake
Lucerne (the lunar image reflecting from which
is said to have inspired the poet Rellstab to give
this sonata is popular name), it is the quiet man
who can rattle off this bit of Beethoven who gets
the girl.

This being a sonata, it actually has three movements, and many commentators have lamented the popularity of the first at the expense of the other two – even Beethoven, who said 'Surely I've written better?' But the first, *Adagio sostenuto*, is where the moonlight lives, and although the musicologist Donald Francis Tovey said 'moonlight will not suffice to illuminate the whole of this sonata', he can whistle Dixie. The second movement is a bit boring and the third is, frankly, a right bastard. But the first might just be possible for a complete beginner.

Moonlight SONATA

'No flamboyant leaps around the keyboard'

Or at least the first bit of the first movement might be. This chapter will equip you to play as far as the second exposition of the famous theme, after which it gets a bit convoluted, to be honest. But by then you should have, to use a proper musical term, scored. If not, you were wasting your time anyway, so feign the need for the lavatory and step away from the piano until a new potential victim appears.

There are several reasons why you should be able to master the first and most important bit of the Moonlight. You know how it goes, so there's no need to become bogged down in trying to make sense of the yellowing and faintly malodorous sheet music from inside the stool. It is rhythmically consistent, the regular *ostinato* triplet figure of the right hand continuing unabated throughout. Meanwhile, the left hand is confined to playing simple octaves and the occasional three-note chord, the middle

note of which can probably be left out for convenience. Part of the Moonlight's continuing appeal with amateur pianists must rest with its relative technical simplicity: there are no changes of tempo, no flamboyant leaps around the keyboard, and it's quite slow. Indeed, most people play it too fast.

And then there's the melody, which, for innocence and naiveté, rivals the One-Note Samba. Textually, it might be transcribed as:

> Dee, de-deeeeeeeeee
> Dee, de-deeeee
> Deeeeeeeeeee
> Deeeeeeeeee
> Deeee, deeee
> Deeeeeeeeeeeeeeeeeeeeeeee

(1770–1827)

Ludwig van BEETHOVEN   Op.27 No.2

Correctly delivered, though, its aching beauty can hardly fail to kindle a fire in the loins of your intended victim, until she is ablaze with inexplicable desire.

There are also one or two problems. That melody is played entirely with the little finger of the right hand, and making it 'sing' demands the ability to use that finger completely independently of all the other digits on the same hand, and regardless of what they might be up to. Since the demise of the mechanical typewriter, few other manual tasks require this particular motor function, so it has been largely lost to mankind. Worse still, and as any anatomist will tell you, the routing of the tendons in the back of the human hand is not conducive to this sort of thing.

So before you even step up to the colossus of iron founding and cabinet making that is the piano itself, practise using your pinky. Place the fingertips of the right hand on a table top, curve the fingers so that the palm of the

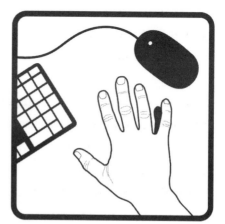

Fig. 1

'You can't play the piano'

hand is parallel with the surface, and, without moving any other finger, try to tap the table regularly with the little one. You can work on this everywhere — office, pub, traffic jam (Fig. 1).

It should also be acknowledged that the Moonlight is in the relatively tricky key of C-sharp minor, which involves a lot of black notes. However, this is only really a problem if you are already learning the piano and your efforts so far have been confined to the easy and largely white-note keys of C, F and G major. If you've never played a piano before, all keys are equally baffling, so in this respect you have an advantage over someone with Grade 3.

Finally, you can't play the piano, but don't let it put you off. With perseverance, this should be possible, with the caveat that this stunt should never be attempted at any event attended by Daniel Barenboim or Andre Previn.

Approach the gleaming, ebony hued *hammerklavier*, as Beethoven would have called it. Or it might be rosewood or walnut, but the point is that where the guitar or the violin is merely a musical instrument, a piano is a piece of furniture and must be overcome as much as played. Do not let the piano sense that you are nervous. Sit squarely at the centre of the keyboard, about half an arm's length away, feet flat on the floor in front of you and within reach of the pedals.

Now, for the purposes of orientation, locate middle C, which in the olden days of piano tuition was usually described as the note immediately to the left of the pair of black notes nearest the lock. Modern pianos generally do not have locks, but middle C will still be, oddly enough, near the middle (Figs. 2a, 2b).

Fig. 2a

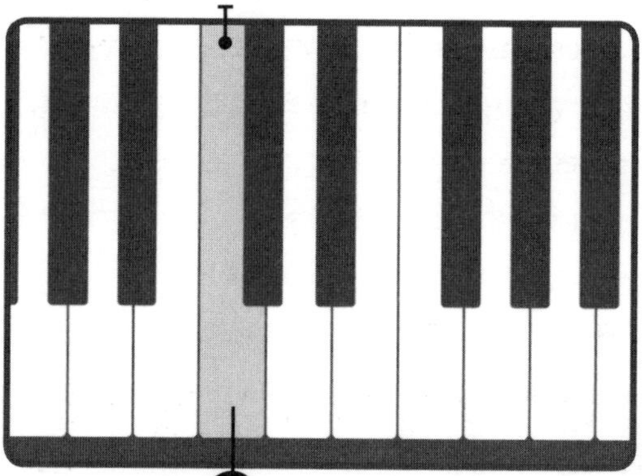

Fig. 2b   **Middle C**

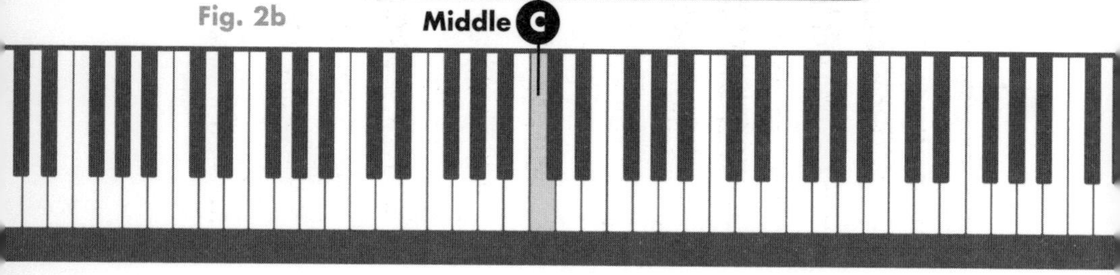

The keyboard will seem immense and incomprehensible; a full-size grand will have 88 keys spanning a breadth of almost five feet. In fact, enharmonically speaking[1] Western music relies on just 12 notes, and if you look you will see that the sequence of seven white notes (A to G) interrupted by five black notes (one group of two, one of three) simply reoccurs seven times as you travel up the keyboard from left to right (Fig. 3).

Any scale you care to name — in this case it's C-sharp minor — uses only seven notes; they are merely repeated as you go up the keyboard but rising in pitch. So high notes are to the right, low ones to the left.

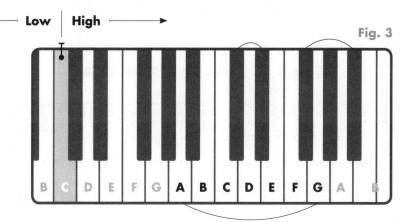

Fig. 3

1 Don't even ask.

Fig. 4

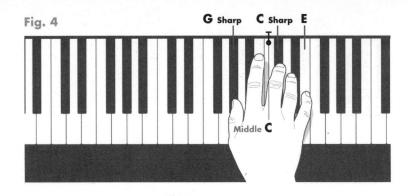

Find middle C again. Immediately to the right of it, and slightly behind, is a black note, C-sharp. Place the middle finger of your right hand gently on this key (fingers bent, wrists and elbows in a straight line).

Now, without moving that finger, place the right-hand thumb on the middle note of the group of three black ones to the left (G-sharp). Finally, place that difficult little finger on E, which is the white note directly to the right of the pair of black notes where we started (Fig. 4).

Play these notes in order from left to right — G-sharp, C-sharp, E — four times and with equal duration. You should recognise something of the opening of the Moonlight (Fig. 5).

Fig. 5

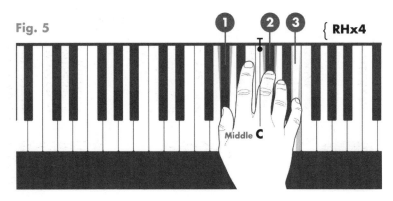

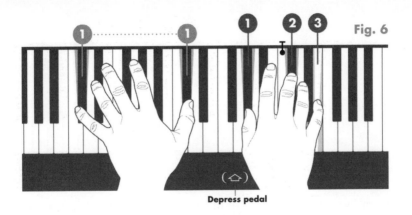

Fig. 6

Depress pedal

Add the left hand. Place the thumb on the C-sharp below the one we have already identified and the little finger on the one below that. Now depress (⌂) the right-hand pedal and play the right hand figure again, but striking the two left hand notes together at the beginning (Fig. 6). You have already performed the first bar of the Moonlight Sonata; or, to put it another way, the first four of just 276 beats making up the entire movement. Have a drink.

The next bar – i.e. the next four beats – is exactly the same as far as the right hand is concerned. The only difference is that the left hand moves down to B, which is the white note to the right of the three black notes below the group of two where your left-hand thumb currently rests (Fig. 7). And as you can probably tell

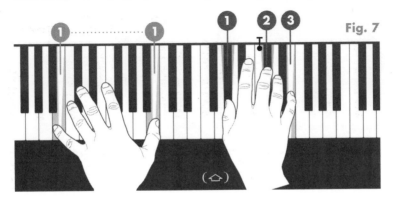

Fig. 7

already, a verbal explanation of the whole movement is going to become about as manageable as transcribing the Old Testament in Letraset, which is why I have devised a diagrammatic aid to learning.

Here's how it works. In regular piano scores the numbers appearing above the notes refer to the fingers to be used on them. In this system the pictures of the fingers indicate which ones to use, and the numbers refer to the order in which they should be played. Notes with the same number should be played together. The (⌒) symbol indicates that you should release and immediately reapply the right pedal.

Remember that the rhythm of the right hand is completely regular, and you will discover that much of it can be broken down into groups of three notes that are repeated up to four times, but sometimes only twice or once.

Real music is divided up into bars, and in the case of the Moonlight they are of four beats each. In this system, the music is divided into individual beats, each one represented by one picture of a keyboard. Read down the page. In the final performance each beat should last for about a second, but go as slow as you like when learning.

Finally, it is important that the diagrams are used in conjunction with a CD recording of the Moonlight, because your ears will guide you better than mere graphic representations ever could, even though that wasn't necessarily true for the composer.

As I can already play this piece, I have no idea how long it will take you to learn it by this method, but I fear it may be a very long time indeed. You may become friendless, destitute and racked by consumption, which is something of a tradition amongst truly devoted musicians. The rewards, though, will be immeasurable.

Although I should warn you that it didn't really work for Beethoven, since Julie Guicciardi gave him the elbow on the grounds of his inadequate breeding and poor prospects, eventually bagging off with a complete count, Wenzel Robert Gallenberg, instead. But he has left nothing to history, while the half-deaf pikey with the piano has bequeathed to you perhaps the most sophisticated and dependable means of seduction ever devised, so you owe it to him to succeed where he failed.

Stick with Ludwig.

Moonlight sonata
EXECUTIVE SUMMARY

1) Fingers bent, arms straight

2) Read down the page

3) Play the notes indicated by the fingers in the numerical order indicated above the fingers.

4) Notes with the same number should be played at the same time

5) The (⌂) symbol indicates that you should release and immediately reapply the right-hand 'sustaining' pedal.

6) Where an indication such as 'RHx4' appears, you should play the same right-hand figure four times, but the left hand figure only with the first one.

7) Listen to a CD first and learn how it goes. Listen for notes that are held, especially in the right-hand melody: these are notated with the **H** symbol. You will soon realise why real music isn't written like this.

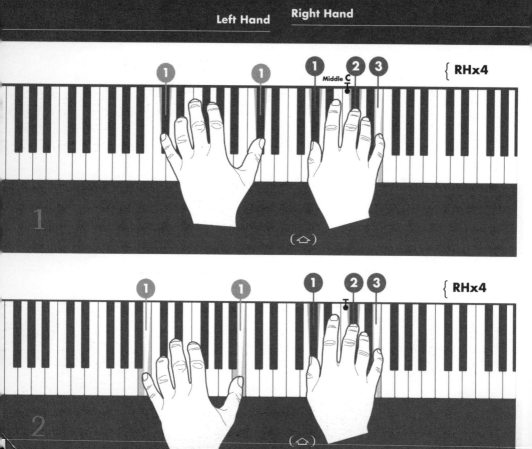

Left Hand   Right Hand

RHx2

RHx2

H = HOLD KEYS DOWN UNTIL LINE 7

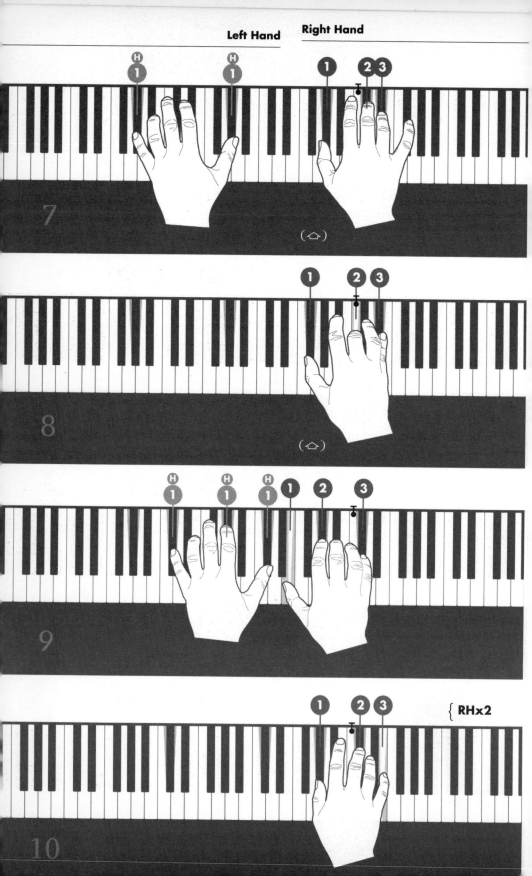

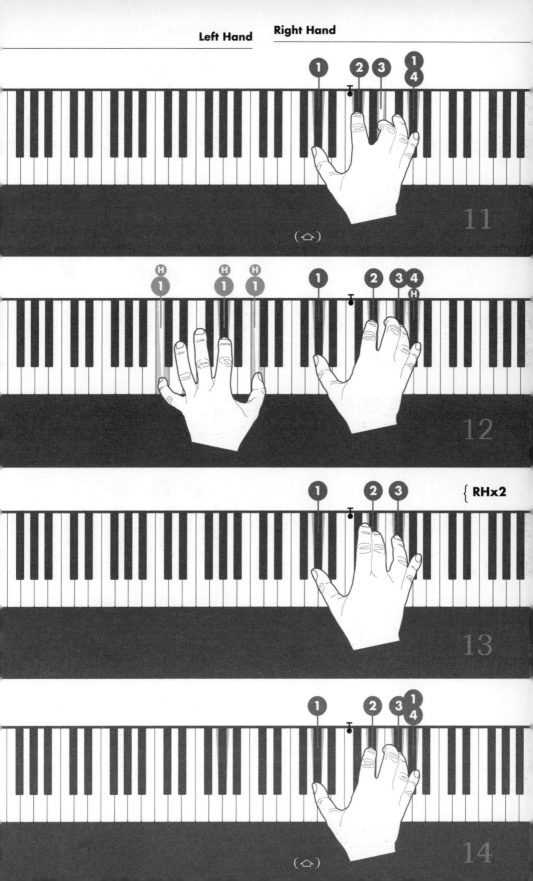

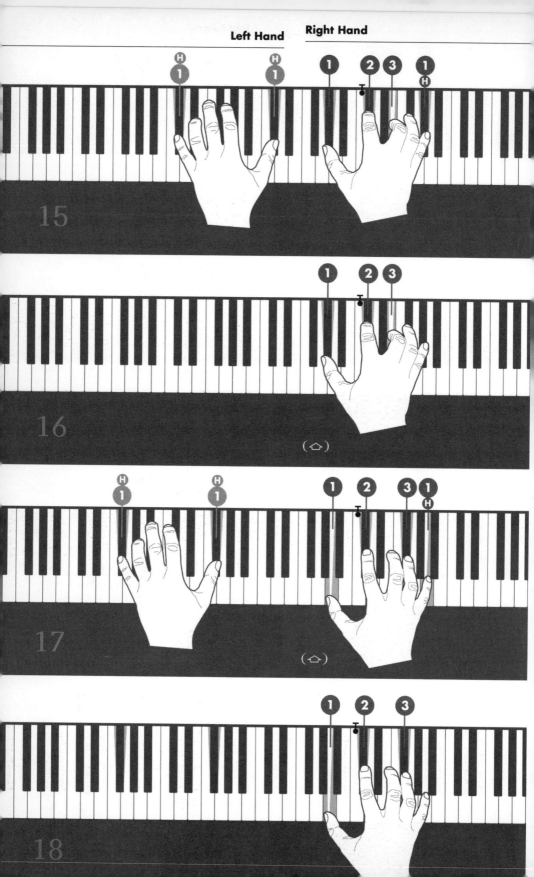

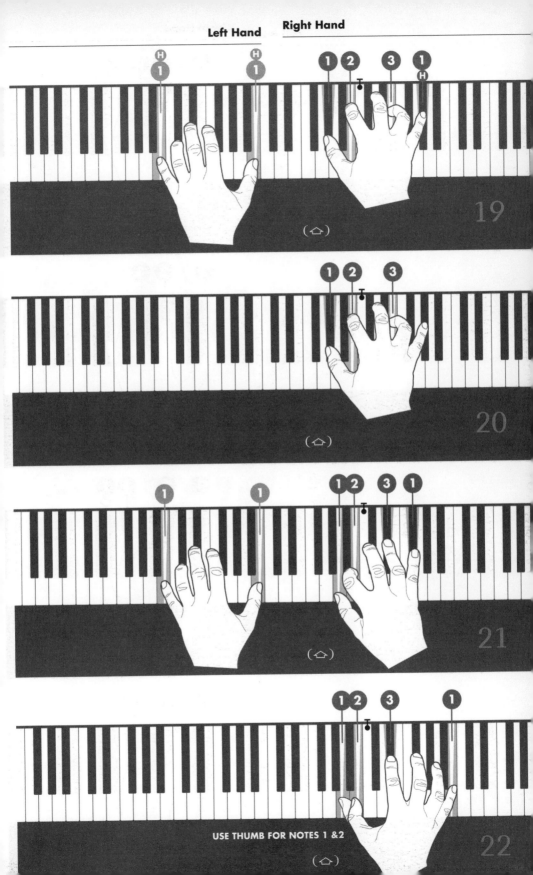

Left Hand   Right Hand

USE THUMB FOR NOTES 1 & 2

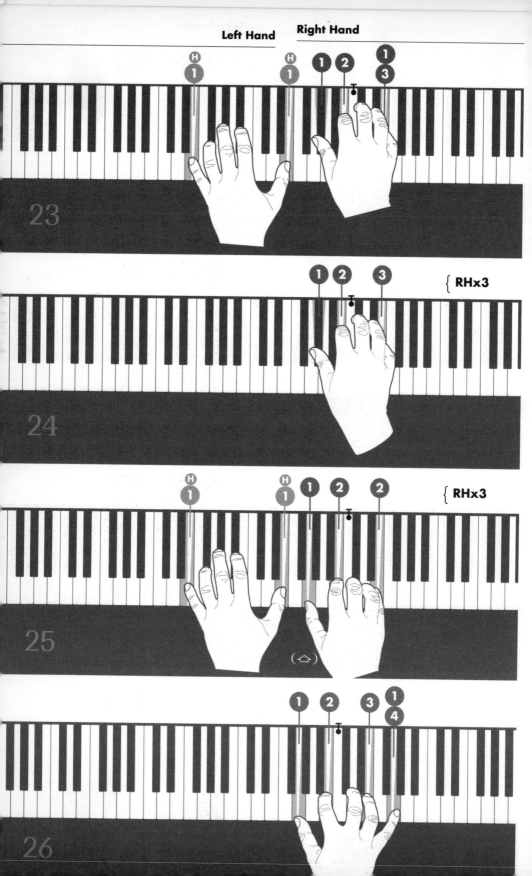

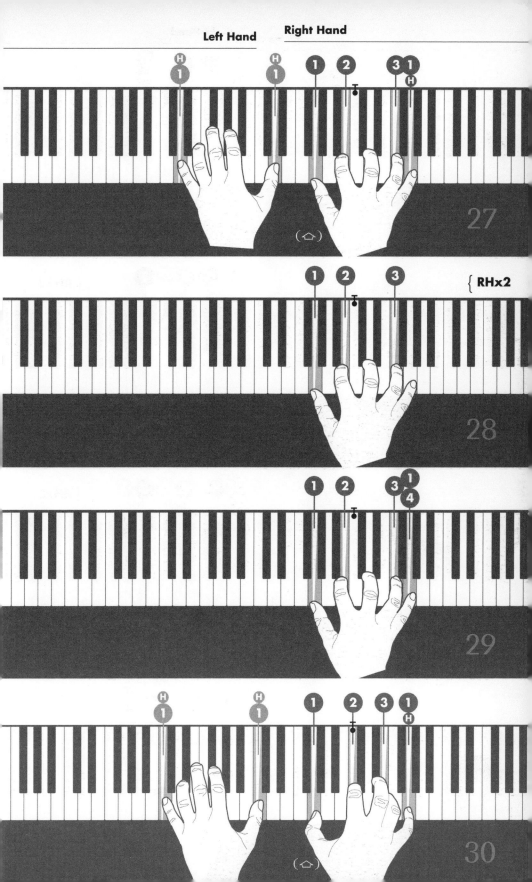

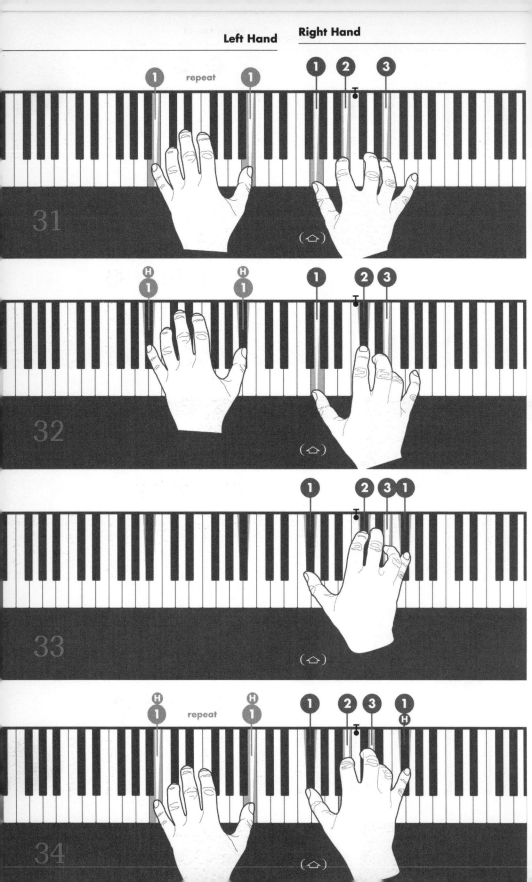

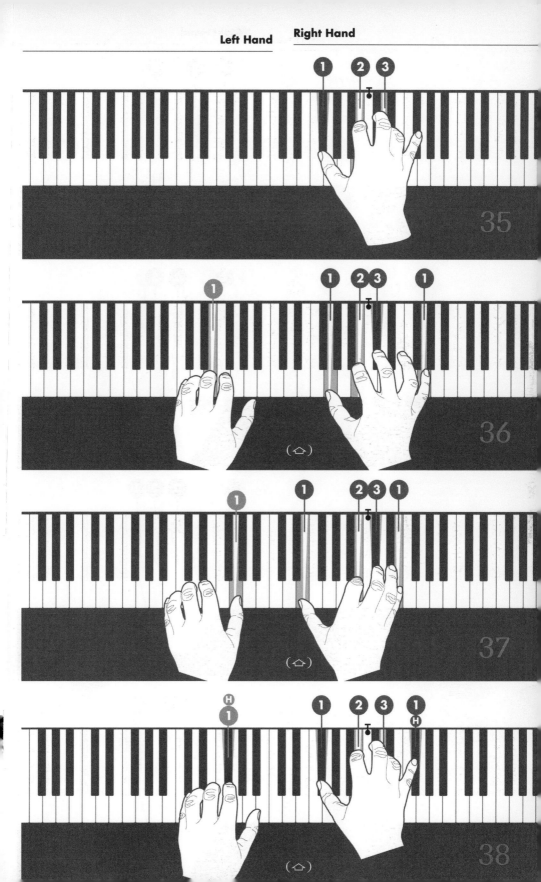

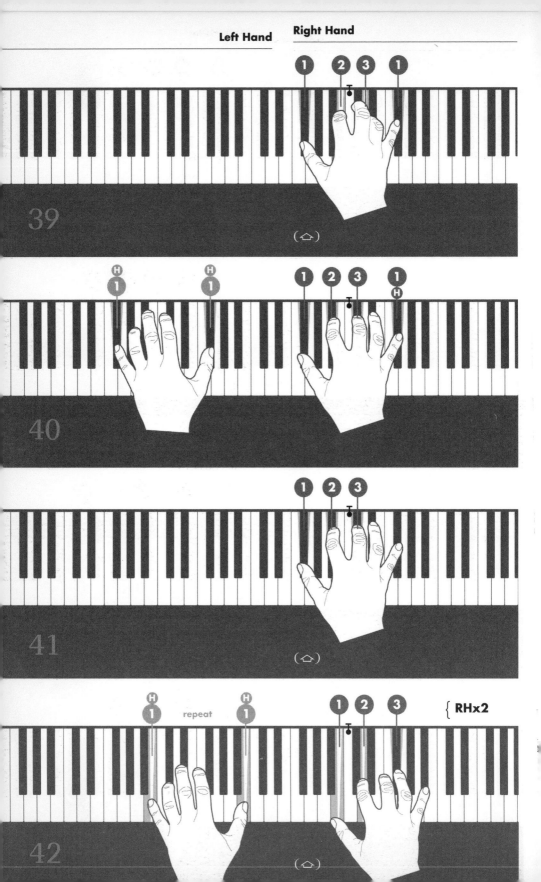

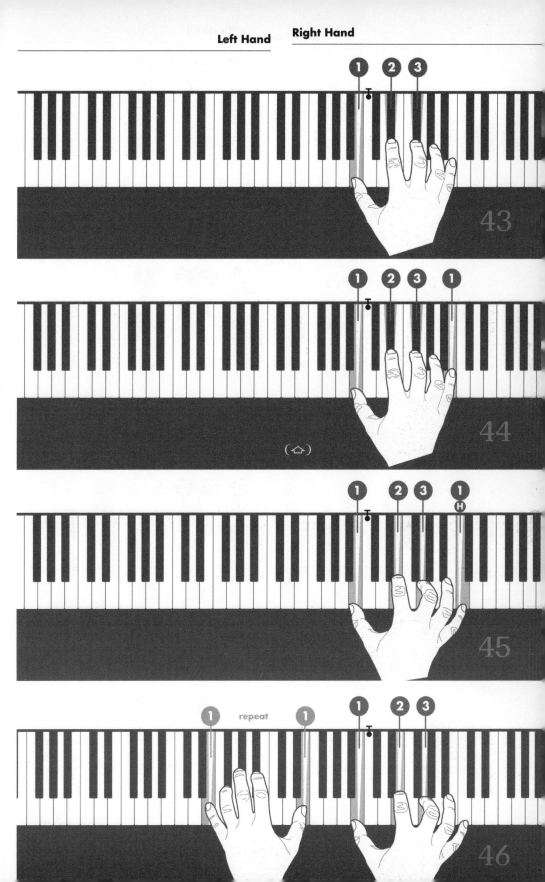

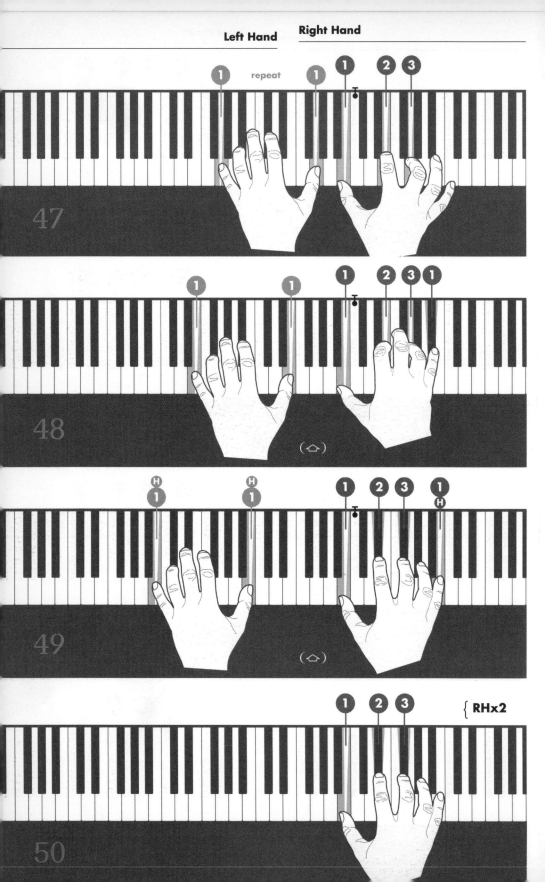

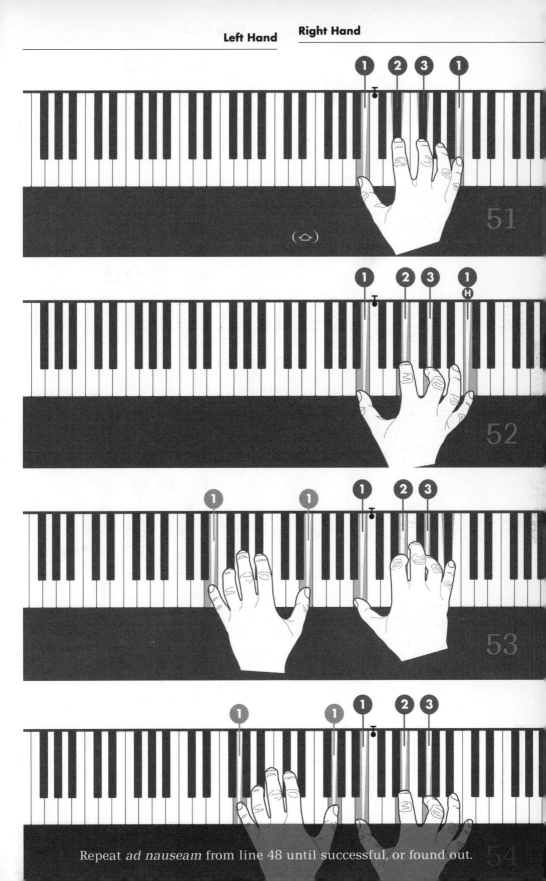

Repeat *ad nauseam* from line 48 until successful, or found out.

ACKNOWLEDGEMENTS

254

With many thanks to, in no particular order:

Airbus

Mike Duff

Dr Chrissie Gardiner

Capt Nigel Rhind

Squadron Leader Dave Parks

Jason Hill

Mark Allatt, John Wilkinson and everyone else at the A1 Locomotive Trust

Isle of Wight Tourist Information

Nick Stroud

Jon Young

Felix Norris

Bobby Birchall

Mike Garland

Cecilia Rushton

Laura Macaulay

Heather Rainbow

Rupert Lancaster

Kate Miles

Rose Alexander

Richard Clarkson

Jeremy Hammond

PICTURE ACKNOWLEDGEMENTS

INDEX